Down to Earth Magic
by Alan Steward

Printed and Bound in the United States of America.

ISBN No. 0-9632646-0-5

Down To Earth Magic

Alan Steward

Contents

Foreword

agic is the oldest science in the world. Yet today nobody seems to believe in Magic anymore. Everything we know evolved from Magic. Chemistry came from the ancient art of Alchemy. Mathematics has its roots in the ancient books of the Egyptians and the Hebrew *Kabbalah*. Today people prefer to trust in machines and technology rather than using the power of their mind.

We are so proud of modern day technology that we don't even realize that we are getting more stupid and ignorant with every generation. We are depending on computers to think for us and ignoring the enormous powers God gave us. Humans were always capable of producing miracles, yet today we depend on machines to provide these "miracles" for us.

There is nothing supernatural about Magic. To practice Magic is every human being's birthright. Now learn how to use the greatest power you posess, the power of your mind.

Magic - The forgotten Language

Magicians have been around for thousands of years. You would find them in the courts of royalty, and they were held in the highest respect. Yet, today people will tell you that Magic doesn't exist. Was everybody in ancient times crazy?

Or is there really such a thing as Magic . . .?

I t is a well known fact that we are only using 5 to 10% of our brain's potential. Isn't it unusual that of all our body parts, only our brain seems to be for the most part useless? Man prides himself on being the only creature on this planet that can think. Yet, he has to admit that he can only use about 5% of his thinking apparatus. Is there any creature on this earth that can't use 100% of the gifts life has given it? Something is wrong here! It just doesn't add up. Do we have a brain that is 95% useless, or did we just forget how to use it?

Most people have forgotten how to use their mind to the fullest. The modern magician's search is for that lost potential. This book is not about metaphysics, spirits, demons, or even God. Whether you believe in them or not has nothing to do with what you will learn from this book.

What you will learn is 100% pure Magic. There is no other word for it. You will find out what I have learned in my lifelong quest for knowledge and the meaning of life. You will find out that Magic is NOT supernatural.

There I was, setting out on my quest for knowledge, with just one fact I was sure of. I did not achieve my full potential in life. I seemed to be stuck with a brain running at minimum capacity, and there seemed to be no greatness in the cards for me. So, what's a man to do? Where do you find the knowledge to access that enormous power hidden away in your mind?

The Subconscious -
The first Breakthrough

hile I was muddeling along with my life, not being too successful in money or in love, I wondered ever so often (just like you), "Why does this guy have all the money?" "Why did this average looking guy marry this beauty queen?" "Why, why, why?" Being blessed with this 5% capacity brain, I could not come up with any explanation. I thought that these people must be extremely lucky or extremely smart. But how do you pin down "luck?"

O ne evening I made a discovery! Actually, this man on TV said he made the discovery. He would tell me all about it, and even sell it to me. It was something he called a "subliminal tape." It was supposed to unlock this secret chamber in my brain called the "subconscious," and transform me into a better person. I could reprogram myself to become thinner, stop smoking, make more money, and many more miraculous things. Was this the secret key to success I was looking for? Well, almost. Subliminal tapes do in a way what Magic does. They do travel into the further regions of the brain and can change a person's "programming."

Let us examine how subliminal tapes work. All of our life our surroundings program us in a certain way. Teachers and parents always tell us what is right or wrong (in their opinion). When we are young, we are told that we are "no good." We will never have this or do that. If you ever were the "fat kid" in school, you know how much bad programming you can get from your peers. The beatings I got from my fellow schoolmates were examples of the finest subliminal programming available today. Time and time again, I was made painfully aware that I was an outsider and not one of them. All this negative information found its way into, you guessed it, that 95% region of the brain where I could not get to it. Believe me, it was there! No matter how much I was consciously aware that I was doing well, and that I was smart and not too bad looking, my subconscious kept on telling me otherwise.

As long as you have negative programming stored in your subconscious, YOU CANNOT BE SUCCESSFUL. This is a hard fact. I don't know anybody who doesn't have at least some negative programming stored away in the far regions of his brain. My guess is that Donald Trump has a whole lot less of it than I did.

There was that miracle cure called the subliminal tape. These tapes have messages recorded so low in volume that your conscious mind can't hear them, but your subconscious can. Therefore, your conscious mind can't argue with the statements on the tapes. If the tape tells you over and over, "you are the greatest," it will be stored right up there with all the beatings you had as a kid. You hope that sooner or later, there will be more "you're the greatest" messages in your brain than fond memories of former beatings.

And here is the catch. There aren't enough tapes in the world to make up for all the bad programming you've gotten as a child. It's like David fighting Goliath (and losing). A little 30 minute tape against 6 years of beatings. You just do not have the ammunition.

Why did I waste your time telling you about those tapes if they do not work all that well? Because those tapes do hold the key to Magic! Magic is a form of subliminal programming (and then some). When you practice Magic, you are not fighting Goliath with a slingshot. You have anything from a shotgun to a Sherman tank in your arsenal, depending on your skills as a magician.

These people on TV really thought they discovered something new and exciting, and they are so proud to tell you about it. In reality, any self respecting high priest on King Tut's court could have told you the secret of subconscious mind programming 4000 years ago. In this day and age of high tech we have more faith in a little 30 minute cassette tape than in the knowledge and wisdom handed down to us from our forefathers for centuries.

We know that King Tut and some of his Pharao buddies had knowledge that still amazes scientists today. How did they build the Pyramids? No builder in his right mind today would even try to attempt such a job.

Let us examine the power of subliminal programming a little further. A magician believes that anything you can think of vividly enough, or conjure up vividly enough in your mind, will eventually really happen. If you can feel and smell that million dollar mansion, and you can see yourself in it without your subconscious giving you any flack, you will get that mansion.

A major university here in the United States has made an amazing study that proved this power of the mind. A group of 90 students was split up into three groups of 30. The first group was taken to the basketball court every day for two hours to practice free-throws. The second group was told to practice free-throws in their mind for two hours daily, but to never actually go to the court to practice "for real." The third group was simply sent home with the message, "Go drink some beer, watch TV. Do what you want, but report back here in one month."

After the one month period was over, all three groups were taken to the basket-ball court to test their improvement in the free throw. The first group, the one that went out on the court everyday, improved nicely, as is to be expected with serious training. The third group, that didn't practice at all, naturally did not improve at all. After all, they were just there for comparison. To everybody's amazement, the second group, the one that practiced their free-throws only in their minds, improved just as much as the first group. Most people who are not aware of the power of the mind, would expect them to do just as badly as the third group.

There is the proof. What you do in your mind (or imagination) is just as effective as what you do in "real life." The important difference is that in your mind, you can do anything. The logical conclusion is that you can do anything your mind can dream up.

I guess the staff at the University of Chicago was very proud of their new discovery, and I am sure a few thousand of your tax dollars paid for the study.

Then again, King Tut's High Priests knew that already. So did the ancient Hebrews who wrote the *Kabbalah*, a collection of books containing a lot of magical secrets we will be discussing later.

Even if you open up the *Bible*, you can find this simple truth. When Jesus was asked about his ability to do miracles, he just answered: *"As I do, so can you."*

Symbolism -
The subliminal tapes
from 4000 years ago

hat other ways are there to get to your programming, your subconscious? Just look around you. You will find the answer on every street corner, everywhere you go. There is a language without words out there. We observe and understand it, without ever really realizing what we are doing.

When you're driving in your car and you see a sign that has a red triangle with a white inside, you know what to do. You yield. When you see a curb painted yellow, you know you will get a ticket if you park there. When you run into the sheriff, you know it's a sheriff. Not because he tells you so, but it's because you see his uniform and his star.

Symbolism is all around us. We react to symbols as well as to words but there is one major difference. We react to symbols on a much more subconscious level. We don't tend to question them as much as words. Somebody can try to tell me that he is with the sheriff's department; without the uniform and that star, there will be little chance he can convince me. We react subconsciously to symbols. This is a rather interesting fact since this is the same way subliminal tapes work.

If you see nothing but Chinese people on the street, sooner or later you will think you are in China. Even if you are pretty sure you are not in China, after a few months without running into an English speaking soul, you at least start to have your doubts. Your belief system starts to crumble, and your subconscious programming begins to be affected.

Now let's go back to the ancient times when the magician was considered the most respected person around, and not the "weirdo."

The first thing we notice when we see ancient artifacts is an enormous amount of symbols. The entire Egyptian language consisted of nothing but symbols. Religion always had its symbols. The Christians have the cross, the Jews have the Star of Solomon. Symbols have been around since Adam and Eve. According to *Bible*, the snake and the Tree of the Knowledge of Good and Evil were the first symbols ever observed by man. Of course you know that they left quite a lasting impression behind. What does all this mean to you, the person who is determined to discover the secrets of life and become a 20th Century magician?

Symbols are the magicians secret language. They are his direct communications link with his subconscious, and as you will find out later with a higher consciousness and ultimately, the forces of nature. You will need patience in trying to make contact with the forces of nature. It requires more than a waive of your imaginary magic wand to be able to do that. In this book, you will find out how to do it, if you really want to. Let us be practical here for a minute, because you want to know what to do with those darn symbols.

I'll give you a simple example of true Magic. Let's assume that you would like to have a beautiful house, well a castle really. You want to go about getting it in a magical way because you are not so sure that you will ever get it any other way.

You feel that you have enough talents and are smart enough to get a house like that, but maybe your subconscious whispers softly in your ear, "Your father didn't have a house like that, your brother doesn't have a house like that, neither does your neighbor. Why should YOU ever get such a mansion?" You probably have a logical answer ready for your subconscious and you might tell it, "Just because my brother does not have a house like that has absolutely nothing to do with my ability to get such a house."

Unfortunately, as you found out earlier in this chapter, there is one thing that your subconscious does not listen to very well, and that is reason. You need to convince your subconscious, that "unused" 95% of our brain that you WILL get that house. How can you accomplish that? You use a symbol instead of reason. Just think back on our episode where thousands of Chinese people showed up in your neighborhood, almost making you unsure of whether you are in China or not. You need something to shake up your belief system in the same way and change your subconscious programming.

You need a symbol representing this house you want so much, and you need to see this symbol wherever you go. Just sit down and think about that house a little deeper. Picture it in front of you. See yourself come up that big circular driveway. You park your car and you turn that big gold doorknob. Hold on, you got it! You might not care whether the house has 5 or 6 bathrooms, or what kind of carpeting you are going to get, but you do want that gold doorknob.

And there is your symbol! Buy that gold doorknob now. Not only will you need it later, (how else are you going to open the door to your big house?) but that big gold doorknob on the mantelpiece right in the middle of your living room will remind your subconscious every day that you need to get that house.

You have put your mind on autopilot. You do not have to argue with it. It already knows, "There is a house missing. It belongs to that doorknob and you better get these two together." You have done a simple magical act.

Not only did you trick your subconscious into accepting that you've GOT to get that house, you have also successfully accessed your subconscious mind. You have accessed the 95% of your brain that wasn't very cooperative before. If you had an IQ of 95 using 5% of your brain, now you are working with a 1900+ IQ potential. Move over Albert Einstein. How hard do you think it is for your new "super brain" to find the means to get that house for you?

The Catch

efore we go on let me state a fact to you — *Magic works. It worked thousands of years ago; it works now. Every time you apply all of your will to get something, magical law says that you will get it. Why are there millions of people who really would like success or riches, but are unable to achieve it?*

Why then, is it possible that you might try that doorknob trick, and it does not work?

Down to Earth Magic *Alan Steward*

or every time you apply your conscious will to get something, there are probably ten occasions when your subconscious will tell you that you CAN'T get it. Let me give you an example. You would like a new car. You use some of the Magic you've learned from this book, and you have a symbol representing your new car hanging in your living room. But when the time comes, you don't get that new car. What went wrong?

Let us examine the day when you worked your Magic a little closer. In the morning you got out of bed and went to buy a "Rolls Royce" key chain. You were all pumped up. Everyday you jingled these keys to remind your "super brain" about the new car. A little later you made a talisman (you will learn about that later), representing your desires for this car you want so much. You've put your all into making it, and you called on all the Gods in the universe to help you get that car. You were really pumped up. Your newly found "super brain" said, "Rolls Royce, Rolls Royce. . . I will get that Rolls Royce."

Now it's lunchtime. You are shuffled around in the lunch crowd and somebody spills orange juice all over you. That's no way to treat a "Rolls Royce Man!" Your magic powers are fading just a little bit.

Later on, your boss chews you out about a report that was supposed to be on his desk by noon. Oh, no! The "Rolls Royce Man" gets treated like the Toyota man he really is! More doubts are creeping up. The "mighty magician" has a hard time in real life. When you arrive home, you find a note that your car payment is late and your rent is overdue. By now, you don't even feel like a "Toyota Man" anymore. You are about to become a "Bicycle Man." That Rolls Royce key chain feels more like a joke than a promise. One morning's worth of Magic destroyed by the troubles of "real life."

Did you just waste your energy doing all that"Magic?" Not at all! I just wanted to make you aware of the destructive effect "reality" can have on your success, with or without Magic. If you bought this book with the hope that all you have to do is waive a magic wand, recite a spell, and all your troubles are over, then you are sadly mistaken. Everything in life takes effort. You will accomplish nothing in life without it. The key to making your Magic work is to become a "true magician." You have to think, act, and feel like the man with the "super brain" you know you are.

Being pushed around in a line will never faze a true magician. On the contrary. Nobody would dare to push around a true magician! Those bills really don't upset you too much if you know with total surety that you will have a Rolls Royce pretty soon. They are nothing but a temporary inconvenience that your "super brain" can easily take care of.

You need to become a total magician. One little symbol or one single magic operation will not help all that much. You need to develop a total magical mindset. I have already shown you some of the principles involved in getting to that hidden region of your mind. If you are ready, fasten your seatbelts and begin your trip into the realm of true Magic.

To be a Magician

We have learned in earlier chapters that whatever your mind can imagine, it can bring into reality. Unfortunately, real life has a way of counteracting our magical operations. We have to learn how to think and act like a real magician. Night and day. We have to grow so strong in our beliefs and powers that "real life" can't possibly bring us down.

Let us examine a little closer what a real magician is all about.

𝕵 f anyone asks you to make a drawing of a magician, I'll bet this is what you will draw: A bearded old man with a long robe, a pointed hat with funny symbols on it, and a magic wand in his hand. He is ready to waive his wand and conjure up something.

This is the picture of the famous Merlin, the wise old man that helped the legendary King Arthur out of a couple of really tight spots. Whether he really existed or not, nobody knows. We do not even know for sure that King Arthur ever existed. Nonetheless, this is the picture people have in their minds when they think of a "real" magician.

So, why the pointed hat? Why the robe? The answer is simple and connects nicely with what we discussed earlier. The magician makes use of symbolism. Here are those magical symbols again. The magician uses his "strange" way of dressing to tell his subconscious, "I am a Magician. I dress like one and act like one. These are not my street clothes. I wouldn't be caught dead wearing this to the office today. There is nothing ordinary about these clothes. Because there is nothing ordinary about me. I am a magician."

This, once and for all, explains why magicians wear strange robes, amulets and headgear. They tell the magician's subconscious that he is about to engage in a magical operation. There is nothing ordinary about him or what he is about to do.

All these little details help you develop a "magical mindset." You are no longer an ordinary person. You are practicing Magic. You know that you are not conjuring up demons or practicing witchcraft. You are simply improving yourself by using all the tricks of the trade your forefathers have been using for thousands of years.

Remember. You are not ever going to wear your magical clothes out on the street. Besides getting you arrested, these clothes would no longer be magical afterwards. This brings us to an important point: Secrecy. Magicians do not practice their craft in secrecy because they are doing something they are not supposed to do. They are not conjuring up demons or the Devil himself. They simply realize that any magical operation that is dragged out into the open will most likely lose its power.

You wouldn't walk around your hometown in a robe and a pointed hat. Surely you can imagine that if you invite your uncle Jed and aunt Frieda the next time you are practicing Magic, their doubts will soon rub off on you and within 15 minutes you will feel like a fool. Bye, bye, Magic! There is no exception to this rule. Magic is to be practiced by yourself. Alone. Even something as simple as buying that gold doorknob to motivate you into getting a new house will invite nothing but ridicule from your friends and neighbors, and the chances for your "Magic" to work are almost nil.

What are the attributes that are needed for your magical workings? A robe is always a good idea, even if it is just a bath-robe. Please don't use the same bath-robe you wear everyday. That robe wouldn't be very special or magical. A true magician would insist that his robe would be either white to symbolize the light of the spirit, or black to symbolize how much he is still groping in the dark for true magical knowledge.

Of course, the robe should be made of a natural material like cotton, silk, or wool. Polyester and Magic do not mix. If you don't wish to spend a lot of money on a robe, just set aside some clothing that you decide to make your "magical clothes." From that point on, you will only wear them while performing your Magic. Now you are dressed for Magic.

The second, and maybe even more important thing you need is a quiet place where you can be undisturbed. This will be your temple. The place from which you will explore the magical universe that is lying behind the blockade called the conscious mind. Concentration is important in Magic. You want to bring success, luxury, or maybe love into your life by ordering your powerful "super brain" to help you in any way possible to get the things you desire. Any disturbance from the outside world will make you wander from your goals.

So, now you are standing in your magical "temple". Which might be the basement, or your bedroom. It really doesn't matter. You are dressed in your "magical clothes," and you really beginning to feel more and more like a real magician. If this room is supposed to be a temple, there should be an altar in it. Let's not stop halfway. If you want to be in a magical mood, you should have something to put your candles on, maybe burn a little incense.

A lot of old Magic books will tell you that it is absolutely essential to have a certain number of candles of a particular color. There also should be incense of a certain kind. It seems that the spirits are drawn to candles and that some spirits like certain kinds of incense. Since you are a practical, "down to earth" magician, you know that it is really your subconscious that you are trying to contact. You should discard these spirits for a while and simply acknowledge that candlelight and the smell of incense will simply put you in a more festive, magical mood.

Now you are ready to do some Magic. You are standing in your temple, wearing your special robe, and really feel like a magician. What to do now? Where are those spells? I guess you are ready by now to speak some magic words and to wait for all kinds of amazing things to happen. I did promise to teach you Magic, but I did not say it was easy. If you could simply recite a conjuration to get whatever you want, everybody would do it. It takes some time to develop a magical mindset, but once you have it, the sky's the limit.

Let us recap what we have learned so far. A magician uses symbols to access the hidden powers of his mind to get him anything he desires. He has to make sure that the stress of his daily life does not bring him down. It could cause him to lose confidence in his abilities. He dresses in special clothing and works in his secret place to reinforce the feeling of "being a real magician". He generally keeps quiet about what he is doing because there is nothing so destructive to your confidence than your friends telling you that you're nuts.

Now we know how to act and feel like magician, let's try some real Magic.

Down to Earth Magic *Alan Steward*

Magic, in theory and practice

Before we get to some practical magical workings, let us examine the principles behind Magic. Why does Magic work? How does it work? What theories did the ancient magicians base their art on? We already know that Magic works by simply "bringing out the best in you." It works by sending powerful symbolic messages to the subconscious mind.

ou already know that the things you do in your mind are as effective as the things you do in real life. But what is the science behind this? All Magic is based on the theory of the Microcosmos and Macrocosmos. The famous magician Hermes Trismegistus said the immortal words "As above, so below."

We find a good example of this theory in the art of astrology. Astrologers believe that the movement of the stars (the macrocosmos) influences people on earth (the microcosmos). Astrologers believe that everything in the universe locks together like a giant machine and that the big wheels (the stars) influence the little wheels (us). If you believe that there is a purpose to us being here and to the universe in general, this makes a lot of sense.

Modern physics starts to confirm this theory rather than disprove it. Everything on this earth, including us, is made out of atoms. If you ever looked into a science book to find out what an atom looks like, you will find that there is an amazing similarity to our solar system. There are little moons, stars and planets buzzing around in every fiber of our body. It just seems to be too much of a coincidence.

Then there is the problem of reality. Is what we are seeing around us only there because we are observing it, or is it there regardless of us? When it comes right down to it, science doesn't have many answers to offer when we ask heavy questions like, "Why are we here? Is the Universe just a big collection of stars and planets or is there some secret plan to it?" Who knows. Our planet earth could be just a tiny part of an atom of a giant dog. We would never dream that something so preposterous could be true until that dog is hit by a truck and our universe suddenly collapses.

Yes, I know, I got somewhat metaphysical on you and I promised not to do that, to keep this book very practical and down to earth. Of course, a good magician has to have his belief system shook up every once in a while, so he does not get into a rut.

We just learned that Magic is based on the "Microcosm - Macrocosm" theory. Everything is connected in some way, so anything can be contacted or influenced in some way. Let's take the metaphysical aspects out of it and examine if there really could be a secret wavelength that our subconscious mind could transmit on. After all, you don't just want to feel and act like a millionaire. You want your boss to feel about you the same way. You want him to feel the need to give you that big promotion you've been hoping for.

If Magic works, and the human mind is so powerful that it can reach out to other people, and make them see things your way, than you are indeed on your way to true miracles.

Let's find a good example that demonstrates how some people's Magic has an effect on other people. Imagine that you work in an office where all your co-workers are in a terrible mood. They had fights with their wives, car trouble, and any kind of bad luck you could think of. Let's also assume that your co-workers are some of the most considerate people you would ever hope to meet. They will not bother you with their bad fortune. They don't complain, and they won't get mean in any way. But still, you are surrounded by a dozen people who just had a horrible day and are pretty depressed. What do you think your chances are that you won't get depressed? Zero, I would guess! The emotions of other people somehow manage to transmit across a distance and they WILL INFLUENCE YOU.

Okay, maybe you'll admit now that you could possibly influence other people's emotions, have them like you (or stay away from you) by "conjuring up" some strong emotions. This is a sort of miracle, true Magic.

Can a magician actually influence solid matter? Can he change an old person into a young person? Can he make it rain? I'll bet you would like me to explain this to you in believable terms, without getting philosophical?

Well, here it goes. Here is an example that everybody has seen in action and it does literally defy explanation. Yet it is a perfect example how your state of mind (Microcosm) can influence your body (Macrocosm).

We have all heard of psychosomatic illness. A person is not really ill, but he feels so bad that he actually makes himself ill. He will have all the symptoms, but it is "not real" Just like Magic. You give him worthless sugar pills, and his symptoms are starting to go away. Some more Magic!

Okay, you can make somebody feel miserable and even give him gallstones without any physical interaction. That sounds more like black Magic to me, and that is surely not what we are after here. Let us try to come up with a more positive example.

We all have heard the saying that a woman in love somehow becomes more beautiful. I have seen this happen dozens of times. Plain old Jane is in love with somebody and her whole face seems to change. That deep down feeling of bliss and happiness makes her face glow and her eyes brighter. It simply makes her look like a different person. Pure Magic! Remember what have we learned about the theoretical side of Magic. You do not need to believe in metaphysics, spirits, or even God to work Magic. The power of the mind is so strong that, theoretically, it CAN move mountains.

We have learned in the first two chapters how the proper mindset can influence you deeply and turn you into a better person. We discussed some examples on how the power of the mind can influence anything around you. There is no limit to what a true magician can do. Most of today's inventions would have been considered Magic just 100 years ago.

We have learned how to communicate over millions of miles through radio waves and telephone cables. Let's throw away our antennas and start doing our "stuff" without the help of electricity.

Down to Earth Magic *Alan Steward*

The Spirit World

ne of the most common statements about magicians is that they have the ability to conjure up and work with entities of the spirit world. That's a statement that definitely doesn't sit very well with today's level headed approach to life. So, what are those spirits the magician conjures up?

Down to Earth Magic *Alan Steward*

o find the answer to this question we need to consider the "Microcosm - Macrocosm" theory again. The spirits are in reality parts of the magicians own personality. By bringing them to life in his imagination, "the Microcosm," he is influencing his mind and the many facets of his personality. Every person has some kind of "split personality." There are so many different facets to your personality. These are the spirits the old magic books are talking about. You can feel mean one day, while on another day you would give the shirt off your back to a stranger.

Here again, we find another metaphysical myth debunked and discover that even in an operation such as conjuring up spirits, the magician in reality works strictly with the power of his mind.

Let us examine the operation of conjuring up spirits a little deeper. Let's assume you are a somewhat shy and you would like to be more aggressive. After all, successful persons are usually "go-getters." And go-getters are usually aggressive in their business practices. Besides, I have never seen a guy make a good impression on a lady by being shy. Now let's have a look inside that ancient spell book that you bought some years ago in the little occult book store downtown, and see if we can get some help from it.

Here is something that ought to work: The Mars spell for courage and aggressiveness. Let us read on, "First you construct a talisman to call upon the Marsian spirits. It has to be constructed in a certain way and painted in a certain color. Then it has to be consecrated (made active) by repeating a spell over it, "O, spirit of Mars, I call upon you in the name of . . . etc., etc. Come into this talisman and give the wearer of it the courage and strength of the ancient warrior."

The kind of spells you find in those ancient books are usually very complicated and filled with strange names like Nachiel, Tzabaoth and so on. People buy these books every day, and try out some of the spells without having the slightest idea of their meaning. Of course they end up achieving nothing. Soon we have another Magic book gathering dust on the shelves. We will not let this happen to this book.

Let's discover the workings behind those spells, find out what the spirits are really made of. When we examine the old Magic spells a little further, one thing immediately comes to mind. What we see described in these old books is just another method of directing your mind with symbolism. The ancient language of Magic shows up everywhere. When we call upon a spirit, we call up hidden strengths (or weaknesses) in the subconscious regions of our mind.

Anybody, no matter how shy he might be, can simply walk up to Miss Universe and ask her out for a drink. We all have that capability. We do know how to say the words, "Hey, let's have a drink." Unfortunately, there are so many road blocks that our subconscious mind has put in our way. When it comes down to it, not more than one out of a hundred persons would dare to walk up to Miss Universe and ask her out.

That power, that personality trait is there, hidden in our mind. By using the proper symbols, like the name of the spirit and his qualities and appearance, we activate that spirit, that part of the personality in our mind without too much interference from our conscious mind. The talisman, or seal of the spirit, that we have created according to the instructions found in the ancient spell book is just another symbol. It tells your mind to release that "spirit," that quality or power you posessed all along. We conjure up a spirit in the Microcosm of our mind to release and activate it in the Macrocosm of reality. Now you know why those spells or talismans you saw in books work (or don't work).

You need to understand what symbols you are working with, and why you are working with them to successfully practice Magic. In later chapters you will learn how to construct your own talismans and spells. You will not simply recite meaningless conjurations and spells. You'll work with symbols and ideas that you can understand.

I am not necessarily saying that spirits do not exist, on the contrary, there might be more things between heaven and earth than you can ever imagine. For our purposes will see these "spirits" as parts of our multi-faceted personalities. If you believe in the existence of spirits, that's fine, but it's not necessary for the practice of Magic.

Energy

*T*here is one thing that makes Magic work, and that is the ability to effectively control energy. What kind of energy are we talking about here? Some metaphysical spiritual energy-form that nobody ever proved really exists?

Well, this is a "down to earth" Magic book; so you will learn about some very real energies that you and I already use in everyday life. These energies are absolutely essential for Magic.

ome people are naturally energetic. They seem to be bursting with energy, and the one thing we notice about most of these people is that they are usually very successful. I have never seen an energetic poor person. Basic enthusiasm and positive energy are absolutely essential to becoming a magician. It is essential to be successful and happy. Period. The truth about any Magic operation is, "You will get out of it what you put into it." If you "sort of" want something, your chances of getting it are slim at best. Put your full energy into anything you want, and anything you do will be "Magic."

The key to everything in this book is energy. Not some kind of mysterious force, but your personal energy, your willpower, strength and enthusiasm. That's the kind of energy you need to practice Magic.

There is a mysterious energy that can connect two people, miles apart, and makes them pick up the phone at the same time trying to call each other. This spiritual energy responsible for "ESP," is nothing more but our "normal" human energy. The person on the other end of the phone called you at the time you needed him because you made "an impression" on him. You made enough of an impression on him (or her) for him to want to call you. If he made an evenly strong impression on you, no wonder you were thinking of calling him, too. Our mind simply works in very predictable ways.

The human mind is, in a way, like a machine. It works in pretty much the same way in all people. It can transmit and receive energy. The energy responsible for ESP or intuition is not supernatural or metaphysical. It is natural human energy. We just don't seem to be able to measure this energy yet with any scientific instrument. Well, there goes the mystery of ESP and that so called "metaphysical" energy connecting us all. Then again, I don't want to bet my life on the fact that there isn't such a thing as psychic energy, or a collective consciousness.

A lot of the magical practices that I'll show you on the following pages will help you train your personal energy. A lot of rituals are designed to strengthen your personal power level, the way you feel about yourself, and the energy level you'll possess. Let's start developing this energy now. In anything you do this week, consciously concentrate on putting just a little more energy into it. Feel a little stronger about it. Show a little more enthusiasm.

The Magical Universe

*I*n order to construct your own spells, you need a road map of the magical universe. You need to know where to find the spirits you are looking for, and you need to learn what kind of surroundings these spirits are comfortable in. In other words, you need to know what kind of incense, colors, and symbols are needed to put yourself into the frame of mind that lets you access the particular spirit, or part of your personality you want to work with.

Let's look at the road map of the magical universe a little closer.

here are four regions in our universe. These four basic regions represent the four elements. FIRE, WATER, AIR, and EARTH. This is the stuff that everything is made of. Everything in this world relates somehow to these four elements, and every idea in your mind has its home in one of these four corners of the magical universe. If you think about these four elements for a minute you can deduct for yourself which elements would be needed for certain spells.

To acquire more confidence and courage, to become a go-getter you would need more FIRE in your life. To achieve security, get a better job, or any kind of material success, EARTH is your natural working place. To acquire knowledge or wisdom and to work with any kind of untouchable, higher concepts, you would find yourself in the domain of AIR. That leaves WATER for any kind of operation involving emotions like love and so many others. Here you have the first and main key to any magical operation.

You want to operate in the proper region of the magical universe in order to be successful. Being a highly sophisticated magician, you know that you just can't repeat FIRE, FIRE, FIRE over and over again. You know that you have to use symbols that represent the particular element you are working with.

The most important kind of symbol you can use is color. There are many books written on color therapy and the influence on color in our lives. Again, science acknowledges these ancient magical theories. The colors for the elements are not really that hard to guess: Fire is red, Water is blue, Earth is brown and/or green. Since we already used up blue for Water, we give yellow to the Air, representing the sunlight that floods the air every day.

To get just a little more spiritual, we also want to call upon the archangels that guard these four corners of the elemental universe. For Fire that would be Michael, and for Air it's Rafael. For Earth we have Auriel, and for Water it's Gabriel. These elements and angels also have an actual physical place in our universe. Earth is in the North, Air in the East, Fire in the South, and Water in the West. We seem to be coming along nicely in our basic spell construction. When we are doing an operation that involves Earth, we should be working with the colors green and brown and invoke the archangel Auriel. Now let's divide our magical universe up a little further.

According to the ancient books of the *Kabbalah* the whole universe (magical or otherwise) is divided into 10 "worlds." These are the worlds we will be working in when we do our Magic. The worlds are: 1 Kether (The Crown) 2 Chokmah (Wisdom) 3 Binah (Understanding) 4 Hesed (Mercy) 5 Geburah (Strength) 6 Tipharet (Beauty) 7 Netzach (Victory) 8 Hod (Splendour) 9 Yesod (Foundation) 10 Malkuth (The Kingdom)

It is interesting to know that the magician will never work in world 1 or 10. The Crown is God, or pure spirit. If anyone would ever be able to make contact with this world, he would no longer need any kind of Magic. On the other end of the scale we find number 10, the Kingdom (Malkuth). That's is our physical earth. Anything we do in daily life is Magic done in Malkuth. So we really have only 8 worlds within our magical universe to consider for magical operations. These worlds correspond to the four elements and also to the astrological signs and planets. In other words, the whole master plan is coming together.

Before I begin explaining these worlds to you, let me give you a little information on their background. The ten worlds were first described in the books of the *Kabbalah*, the secret Hebrew textbooks that, some people say, actually pre-date the *Bible*. The *Kabbalah*, or Quabala as it is also sometimes called, is the background of any Magic book ever written. Even in today's witchcraft rituals you will find many kabbalistic influences. The books of the *Kabbalah* are really not Magic books at all. There are no spells in it. There isn't any mention made of conjuring up anything.

The *Kabbalah* is a blueprint of the magical universe. It is a dictionary of symbols and symbolism that lets you classify and access any "spirit" or any idea that you can think of.

To get in the proper mood for a certain magical operation, everything in your temple should be somehow related to the magical world or sphere you are trying to access. The colors you use should be right. The smell of the incense must be correct. The names of God, angels, and spirits you are trying to contact have to be correct. So, let's have a closer look at our road map.

Let's take a trip around our magical universe and examine the magical worlds a little closer. Our first stop upward from Malkuth, the "real world" is:

YESODE

The Foundation. Its number is nine. This is what a lot of people call the astral plane. The world of creation. This is where ideas are born. The planet governing this sphere is, naturally, the moon, our closest relative. Its color is violet, silver is the metal, quartz the stone, Jasmine the scent and Sha-dai El-Chai the name of God that rules this sphere. In this sphere you will find the Kerubim and Archangel Gabriel. As you can see from these correspondences, this is the sphere where our new age friends are right at home, we find the moon here, and the quartz crystal. This is the psychic world. The next world is:

HODE

Splendour. The eighth world of the Kabbalah. We are visting this world in all magic operations that have to do with the sciences, wisdom, and knowledge. In this world, Mercury rules and the color is orange. The scent is Storax; the name of God for this world is Elohim Tzavaoht. The Metal and Stone are Mercury and the Fire Opal. The Archangel here is Michael and the Angels ruling here are called Beney Elohim, the Children of God. We find them in Genesis Chapter 6. The next world we are visiting is:

NETZACH

Victory. This is the sphere of Venus. Naturally, this is where your love spells are to be handled. The color is green, and the scent is that of the Rose. Copper and Emerald are the metal and stone of choice here. Its number is seven. Yod-He-Vau-He Tzavaoth is the appropriate God name and Archangel Haniel and the angels named Elohim (The Gods) rule here. Now let us move up to world number 6:

TIPHARET

Beauty. The scent common in this part of our magical universe is Olibanum and gold is the metal and color of choice here. This luxurious world is ruled by Yod-He-Vau-He Elohah Vadaath together with Archangel Raphael and the angels called the Malachim. You can pretty much guess that the sun rules this sphere. Further up on the list of kabbalistic worlds we will find:

GEBURAH

This means strength. Its number is five. It is the domain of Mars, and tobacco is the scent of choice. The color is scarlet red and Iron and the Ruby are the appropriate Metal and Stone. Elohim Gibor is the name of God in these parts, and the Archangel Khamael (meaning the severity of God) and the Seraphim (the fiery serpents) rule here. It's a man's world up here. To receive courage and strength, there is no better world to construct your spells in. If you are looking for money, you want to visit:

HESED

Blue is the color, four is the number, and the warm smell of cedar fills the air. Jupiter, the planet connected with financial success, rules together with the God El, Archangel Tzadkiel and the Angels named Chasmalim (the brilliant ones). Tin is the metal used around here and the Sapphire the appropriate stone. We have covered the lower worlds of the Kabbalah and we are now moving on to the lofty, spiritual world of:

BINAH

Understanding. The Color is black. (Remember the symbolism of our black robe, meaning "we haven't learnt anything yet.") The scent is Myrrh and the planet of Saturn rules here. The number is three. Yod-He-Vau-He Elohim rules here together with the archangel Tzaphkiel (The contemplation of God). The angels are called Aralim. The metal is lead and the stone is the pearl. (Pearls of Wisdom, get it?)

Isn't it amazing how the symbolism in our magical universe comes together and starts to make sense? Well, we only have one world left in our travels and that is:

HOCHMA

Wisdom. Understanding leads to wisdom. This is the highest a mortal soul could possibly travel and only the loftiest operations are performed up here. Gray is the color, the medium between the white brilliance of KETHER and the Black of BINAH. Two is its number. Musk is the Scent and Yah the name of God. The Star Ruby and Turquoise are the stones and there is no metal. Ratziel is the archangel ruling these spheres, and the Auphanim are the angels in charge of these parts of the magical universe.

This concludes our short trip around the magical universe. We will learn more about these magical worlds later. Right now, let me recommend some additional reading material to you. First of all, you might have already deducted that the names of these magical worlds and their inhabitants are all in ancient Hebrew. Any book that discusses the *Kabbalah* in detail will not only tell you more about these magical worlds and their inhabitants, but will also help you with the proper spelling of the Hebrew names found in this book. Some of the writings of the Golden Dawn are good study material, and a simple Hebrew dictionary will help also.

Let me give you just two guidelines on pronounciation here. The letters CH are pronounced in a very sharp manner, almost like you are clearing your throat. The letter I is pronounced like the ea in "read." This will get you through most of the Hebrew names. Michael would be pronounced like Mee-cha-el. Elohim like A-low-heem.

By proper use of the 10 worlds of the Kabbalah you can construct any spell and do any magical operation, including the making of talismans and amulets. In a later chapter you will learn how to do basic spells and how to construct talismans for any purpose.

You might be wondering about all this symbolism and whether or not your mind is able to file all these symbols into their proper places. How do you know that Emerald Green is indeed the proper color for a magical operation to bring love? Believe me, your subconscious will recognize these symbols and react accordingly.

These magical attributions have been developed over thousands of years, and found proven to work and to activate the proper area of your subconscious. Now we are just about ready to perform some real Magic. Let's take it easy for a while and let all that newly found knowledge sink in. Let's do some "Easy Magic."

Easy Magic

ou have learned the basic principles needed to work Magic, and why Magic works. Now it's time for me to share some of my experiences with you and share some simple techniques that always seem to work. They seem so simple that you may not even call them Magic.

Please don't be fooled by their simplicity. These techniques are very important for your development as a magician. Without regular practice of these techniques you will, at best, become a mediocre magician. On the other hand, these "Easy Magic" techniques might be all you ever need in life.

I know the exercises in this chapter are not all that glamorous. There are no "spirits," and no difficult conjurations to recite. What you will learn in this chapter are the basics for your development as a magician. If you can master these "Easy Magic" techniques, you will have what it takes to call yourself a magician.

Magic Trick #1 — Give a little, take a lot

This is what is called the law of tenfold return. Give a little of your money for a good cause, a charity, a needy person, or your church and you will get ten times as much back. It is like the pay-out from the cosmic lottery. There is no Ed McMahon here, telling you that you MAY have already won. The magical wheels are already in motion and invariably, you will get your reward.

Churches call this tithing. You will give 10% of your income to the church and in return, you will receive so many monetary blessings that a measely ten percent doesn't even seem to count. These infamous TV preachers are trying to sell you on this principle every day, 24 hours a day. Just send them the money, and you will be blessed with more than you ever gave in the first place.

Remember, the law of tenfold return says, "Give something to the needy people and you will get back ten times as much." If you can show me a needy TV preacher, I would gladly give him some of my money. If not, it's better to approach a homeless person, help a neighbor in need, or to contact the Salvation Army. Well, let's see this law of tenfold return in action.

Here is all you have to do. The next time you give a 10 dollar donation to the Salvation Army, just say to yourself, "I have just received a hundred dollars and I thank you." Don't "try for more." Don't say, "I have just received 1000 bucks." The law is called the law of TENFOLD return. It does not mean that you might not get more than a hundred dollars, but you don't want to be greedy.

I have seen this principle work too many times. I don't know how it works, but I would bet my life on it. It seems to work every time. I might give 20 dollars to the Leukemia Society and three days later I receive a 200 dollar order from a brand-new customer that I never dealt with before. I recommend you don't just take my word for it, try it for yourself.

Magic Trick #2 — Mental Magic

*T*he power of the mind is really all you need to do Magic. The more proficient a magician you become, the less trappings and gimmicks you need to make your Magic work. The ultimate magician only has to utter a word and whatever he wants comes to pass. Of course, you (and I) are a long way from that kind of mind power. Here are two very simple forms of mental Magic that in a lot of cases will do the trick for you.

The first one is a little magical mini ceremony. Sit back and try to relax yourself as much as you can. If you know how to meditate, do that. If not, just imagine your body relaxing piece by piece, starting with your feet and working your way upward to your head. Then imagine a pure white light descending upon your head and slowly covering you completely. There is some obvious symbolism in the white light. You want to forget all of your day to day activities, and the colors that you see in every day life. Concentrate on the pure white brilliance of your spiritual self. This brilliant white light will help you get into a "magical mood."

Now you are ready to do your actual Magic. Concentrate on what it is you want until you actually experience it in your minds eye. If you want a new car, see yourself driving it. Smell the new leather. Make it as real as your can. Concentrate and build up the energy of your will. Say to yourself, "I WILL HAVE THAT CAR!"

When you feel the energy building up to a climax, imagine that, without a shadow of a doubt, your will just made whatever you wanted happen. Feel the whole universe bend to your will for a split second to adjust to your desires. Then firmly say, "It is done."

That's it. You have just performed a Magic spell, the purest form of a Magic spell. If you trained yourself to the point that you really feel like a magician, as discussed earlier, your wish (command) will indeed be fulfilled.

Magic Trick #3 — The free Caribbean Vacation

Stress is a serious health hazard. Besides the damage it can do to your body, it surely doesn't help in your quest to become a true magician. Not everybody can afford to take a Caribbean vacation every time he wants to. Then again, nothing is impossible for a true magician. Let me show you how you can travel to the exotic island of your choice. Anytime you wish, and without the need for a plane ticket or a passport.

For this you need to learn a little bit about self-hypnosis. Actually, you have already done some self-hypnosis when you tried the little mini ceremony in your mental Magic exercise.

The practice of feeling you body relax one part at a time is the basic technique used by every hypnotist. When you imagine yourself surrounded by the white light your relaxation will increase also.

Let's go over the entire process of self-hypnosis in more detail. First of all, sit or lay down and make yourself comfortable. Do not make yourself too comfortable, or you might fall asleep. Before you start with the actual relaxation, do some deep breathing. Breathe in, count to 4, breathe out. Do that about 6 times. Then let the white light come down your head and let it cover your body just like in the mini-ceremony.

Now you are ready to imagine your feet getting all relaxed and tingly. (The tingling really helps. Just try it.) Now relax your calves, your ankles, and so on, until you finally finish all the way up in your scalp. Now imagine yourself going down a staircase. There are twenty steps on your imaginary staircase and you are counting backwards as you go down. 20 - 19 - 18 etc. Make sure you are really feeling yourself go down! Once you are down the stairs you are actually in a state of hypnosis.

Most people will feel absolutely normal and very much awake in this condition, like "nothing happend." This is fine for our purposes. As you practice this more often, you will feel that your relaxation increases every time you do this exercise.

Now let's get back to our staircase. At the bottom of the staircase you will find a door. Imagine this door with as much detail as you can. See the color and the type of wood it is made of. Now you are ready to take a trip to your very own paradise. Wherever you want to go, your favorite place is right behind that door. It can be a real place like Hawaii, the Bahamas, or maybe the mountains. It could also be a place of pure fantasy.

By creating your own fantasy paradise you will exercise your magical imagination. You could put yourself into a pre-historical rainforest where dinosaurs and bisons roam. Maybe you can place yourself into the heavens of the greek Gods and have tea with Zeus and flirt with Aphrodite. You will be amazed what kind of journeys you can take and what amazing adventures await you behind that imaginary door.

Once you feel your vacation has lasted long enough, turn around and go through that door again. Close the door and know that your paradise will be there when you return. Then go up the stairs and count from 1 to 20 while going up. Once you are at the top of the stairs you will find yourself totally relaxed and ready to face the real world again.

Magic Trick # 4 — Magical Workouts

hen you do Magic, you work with your sixth sense, the hidden regions of your mind. Everyone on this planet had some experience with premonition and unexplainable "coincidences" before. Our mind's ability of receiving and transmitting energy is what we call ESP or the sixth sense.

Developing this sixth sense (which is part of the unused 90 to 95% portion of your brain) is what Magic is all about. A magician, just like an athlete, will want to do a daily workout to train and increase his newly found powers. The magical vacation described earlier is a great workout, but let's try something that lets us keep score.

You have probably seen so-called ESP-Cards. One has a triangle, one has a circle, and one has a square or some other symbol on it. The idea is to guess the symbols on the cards without looking at them and then to keep score. For us aspiring magicians, this method is a little too crude. After all, we are working with subtle ideas and energies, and we need a more accurate method of finding out how good our ESP-Quotient really is. What does a true magician use? Most likely a Tarot Card deck. Since you might not have one of those and we haven't discussed Tarot Cards, let's use a regular deck of playing cards for now.

Let's look at the different symbols and possibilities. There are two colors, four suits and 13 different numbers or figures. This will help you keep score of whether you are almost right, close, or very close. To guess the right color is a fifty-fifty proposition and we will ignore this. If you guess the right suit AND the right number or suit, give yourself 10 points. If you have Queen of Hearts and you said Queen of Hearts, that is a perfect score and in theory, that should only happen once every 52 times. If you have the number or symbol right, give yourself 5 points and if you only have the suit right (a one in four chance) give yourself 2 points.

Besides just getting right or wrong answers, you can determine if you are "getting warmer." If you start to pick up on the ideas and combinations in the cards rather than just Yes or No possibilities, you can chart your progress much more accurately. I recommend doing this exercise every day, and you will surely see your scores improving.

Why did I list this mental exercise under the heading of "Easy Magic?" The development of your intuition will help make Magic easier for you more than any other practice described in this book. You are honing your magical skills. If you start listening to your intuition you will suddenly make more and more "right" decisions. You will automatically know what to do. You will "feel" it when a person is lying to you. You will also find yourself more than once in "the right place at the right time." Your intuition will do more for you than you ever imagined.

Please remember, it's of no use training your intuition and then ignoring it when the time comes. Start listening to your "inner voice." If something inside you says, "do this," then do it. You won't make a mistake by following your heart.

These very simple practices you have just learned will help you make great strides in your quest to become a true magician. If you feel you're ready, let us delve somewhat deeper into the magical world and learn how to perform a magical ceremony and how to construct our magical tools, talismans and amulets.

Magic Rituals

*A*re you ready to conduct a full blown magical ceremony?

If you did the exercises discussed in the earlier chapter and are thoroughly familiar with the magical worlds, you have most of the knowledge to work some "Real Magic." The first thing we will learn is not only a ceremony in itself, but it will also be part of any other ceremony you'll ever do. It is called a banishing. No, we are not banishing or exorcising evil spirits or demons.

A banishing will "clear the air" from all negativity that surrounds you.

𝕵 f you have negative people around you, whether at work or in the home, you just can't help but feeling depressed yourself. What you need is an effective shield against negativity. The method I am about to describe has been used for hundreds of years and is proven to be one of the best defenses against any kind of negative influences. Regular practice of these banishings will make you a more balanced person. You will not get upset that often and you will be, in general, a happier person. Any self respecting magician will do his banishings at least once a day and would not dare to miss it even for a day.

The banishing you're about to learn comes from the teachings of the Golden Dawn, probably the most influential magical order that ever existed. The Golden Dawn was active in the late 1800's and early 1900's and brought forth some great translations of famous Magic books that before that time only existed in ancient languages. The Golden Dawn called this ritual the "Lesser Banishing Ritual of the Pentagram" or LBRP for short. From the name you can deduct that there also must be a "Greater Ritual," but for our purposes, the LBRP will do just fine.

If you want to learn more about the Golden Dawn and their rituals, there is a book out that you might want to study. It's called *The Golden Dawn* by Dr. Israel Regardie, one of its former members.

Please be forewarned. This 1000 page book is heavy fare. It is not very easy to understand and a good background in Magic is required. (I certainly hope to give you at least a little of it in this book.)

Let us look at the LBRP close-up. First of all, it is highly recommended to take a very leisurely bath before doing any Magic. This will not only relax you, but you are also symbolically washing away the troubles of daily life. If you have some scented bath oils, use these to enhance the atmosphere you want to build up. Real magicians will use the scents appropriate to the area of the magical universe they are working in. In other words, if you are getting ready to conduct a love spell, you would use rose scented oils or perfumes in your bath. Here is another reason why you have to know about the magical universe and its correspondences.

In most occult or curio shops, and also some health food stores, you will find a wide selection of essential oils. These oils are very pure. A rose or jasmine oil will have nothing but rose or jasmine in them, while most commercial perfumes are mixtures of different scents.

Let's get out of your bath and put on your magical clothing. Make yourself feel like a true magician. Proceed to your secret working area, your temple. Make sure you will not be disturbed. Unplug the phone and tell your wife, neighbor, brother or roommate to leave you undisturbed for 30 minutes.

Be sure to create a nice "magical" atmosphere in your temple. Don't use electric light. Light some candles. Also, burn some incense. Now you're now ready to begin.

In the LBRP you will work with the four basic regions of our magical universe, the areas of Fire, Water, Air and Earth. You will start the ceremony by doing a little mental Magic first. Stand in the middle of the room facing East and imagine that you are ascending into the sky. Some people can do this with their eyes open, others can only do this with their eyes closed. Whatever works best for you is fine. You might want to start out with closed eyes and as you get more comfortable you can open your eyes to soak in the magic surroundings you have created around you. See the candlelight and take in smoke from the incense.

As you are going on your mental trip up into the sky, see your hometown under your feet getting smaller and smaller, then actually see the earth getting smaller and smaller. You will pass by the moon and eventually end up in the center of the universe. This is your place of operation. You, the magician ARE the center of the universe. If you do this often enough, you can instantly switch yourself to the center of the universe. In reality, wherever you are, IS the center of the universe.

Now imagine a bright white light over your head. This is the same cleansing spiritual light that we encountered in our self-hypnosis session. Lift up your hand and actually grab the light and drag it downward to where your head is and say the words AH-TAH, drag it down to a point just below your waist and say MALKUTH (Malkoot) then bring it up to your right shoulder and say V-GEDULAH then over to your left shoulder and say V-GEBURAH. Now move your hand (and the light) to your chest and say LEE-OHLAM AMEN. You have just formed a cross of bright, spiritual light inside your body. The cross was actually a spiritual symbol long before Christianity. It goes back to ancient Egypt. Also note that the lines on this cross are all of equal length. This is called the Kabbalistic Cross.

Now point your finger eastward and draw with it a five pointed star in the air according to the diagram pictured here. This star is also made out of pure white-blue radiant light. A lot of people think that the five pointed star or pentagram is some kind of evil symbol. In reality, it symbolizes the rulership of the spirit over the lower elements. The lower four points of the star symbolize the four elements: Fire, Water, Earth, and Air. The top point represents the spirit or God.

Fig. 1
The Pentagram

When we draw the pentagram in this particular ceremony, we always start at the lower left corner. This is the corner ruled by Earth. As lowly, beginning magicians, we will be mainly concentrating on banishing negative influences right here on our earthly plane. Remember to draw this pentagram in the air with its point facing up, symbolizing the rulership of the spirit over the elements. If you turn this symbol upside down, with it's single point facing downward, you get the evil symbol you might have seen in some movies about black magic or satanism.

The symbolism here is obvious. An inverted pentagram shows the lower elements ruling over the spirit. Of course, whoever values material things over spiritual things is. . . .a yuppie (or maybe a satanist)? Please make sure your pentagrams point upward. (Who wants to be a yuppie anyway?) It doesn't matter whether you can picture this pentagram very vividly in your mind or not, this will come with time. It will suffice that you KNOW you have just created a pentagram up there.

Now move your left foot forward and point to the pentagram in front of you with both hands and say loudly **YOD-HE-VAU-HE**. We have already learned about the God names that rule different parts of our magical universe and this is one of them. Now slowly move your finger toward the South. Leave your finger up in the air. Do not lower it. The light should CONTINUE coming out of your finger while you are tracing a line to the South. When you face South, trace another pentagram. Put your left foot and both arms forward and say **A-DO-NAI**.

Continue the line to the West, trace your pentagram, foot and arms forward and say **EH-HE-YE**. Then continue the line to the North, trace your pentagram and say **AGLA**. After that, continue tracing the line until it connects with the pentagram in the East that is now in front of you. You have just created a MAGIC CIRCLE. The line connecting all these pentagrams forms a circle around you, and the protecting pentagrams, activated by the God names are guarding the four corners of your magical universe.

Now concentrate for a while on the mental image you have just created. There is a white cross of light inside your body and a circle of light around you. There is also a glowing five pointed star in each corner of the room. Remember, this is not your room anymore; you are standing in the center of the universe. One just can't help but feel just a little more powerful and more balanced contemplating this. Concentrate on strengthening the light around you. Let the circle around you surround you with brilliant light, protecting you from anything earthly that might be able to bring you down.

Now look toward the East and picture a towering figure dressed in yellow in front of you. Remember, East is the domain of the element of air and yellow is the color of air. The archangel ruling air is Rafael and this is the figure you see before you. Feel the air rushing out of this corner and say, "before me, **RA-FA-EL**."

Now picture a figure dressed in blue behind you. Keep facing east and simply FEEL him standing behind you. Say, "behind me, **GA-BRIEL**." Behind you, in the quarter ruled by water stands the archangel Gabriel. Now say, "to my right **MI-CHA-EL**." See the archangel of Fire standing in that corner, dressed in scarlet red. Say, "and to my left **AU-RI-EL**." There in the corner of Earth and dressed in brown and green stands Auriel, archangel of Earth.

Next, picture a big brilliant pentagram surrounding you and say, "for about me the flames of the pentagram." Then picture a small, golden six-pointed star above your heart and say, "and within me the six-rayed star." Now do the Kabbalistic Cross again and you are done.

If you want to, you can contemplate for a while that wonderful imagery that you have created. There is one point I have not yet mentioned, and that is the special method that a magician uses to say the names of the Gods and archangels.

You might have noticed that I bold-faced these names to have them stand out. The reason for this is that these names should be said with force. I do not suggest that you should scream, or even say them very loud. There should be a certain strength in your voice when you say the names. You must FEEL that your voice reaches all the way to the depths of the universe when you say these names. After all, you are talking to Gods and you are invoking archangels here. That is no small order.

Let us examine the ritual we have just completed a little further. What have we done here? To start with, we have spiritually cleansed our surroundings with the white light. We have built around us a fortress of protective pentagrams sealed by the names of God. To top it all off, we have invoked the archangels to help and protect us. Besides the obvious beauty of this ritual we are telling our subconscious that we ARE the center of the universe. We can shield ourselves from all negativity, and we even have the archangels at our disposal any time we want them. Not only is this banishing the basis of any other magical operation you will ever do, you will also find that IT REALLY WORKS WONDERS.

You will strengthen your defenses against negativity, you will feel and be happier and your friends and co-workers WILL notice the difference. The inner light you created with the Kabbalistic cross and pentagrams actually doesn't completely disappear when you finish your ritual. A little bit of it will stay with you, and every day a little more of it will "light up your life."

I recommend highly that you do these banishings every day. Once you have this ritual memorized, it won't take more than maybe 10 minutes of your time and it will make an enormous difference in your life.

By the way, there is no reason why you couldn't do this ritual in your imagination. Remember what we have learned in the beginning of this book. Anything you do in your mind will be just as effective as what you do in "real life." There are some advantages and disadvantages to doing this ritual "in spirit" only. The obvious advantage of doing a ritual in your mind, of course, is that you can do it anywhere, at any time. The disadvantage is that it will require a lot more concentration from you. If you are a beginning magician, you will like the impact that your candles and incense make on you while doing your Magic. It is easier doing something "for real." You can smell the incense. You can touch your robe, and see the altar in front of you.

It is also hard to re-create something in your mind that you haven't done very often. As a beginning magician, you should always do physical rituals.

Once you are advancing in your magical prowess, you can start with some banishings in your mind. Once you have become the master magician you always wanted to be, you do not physically have to do any magical operation anymore.

Remember, it's all in the mind.

More of the Magical Universe

Before we can move on to some of the more practical operations, like the love and money spells, we need to learn a little more about the 10 magical worlds.

I know that's what you bought this book for. To be able to get all the love and money in the world, right? There are more love and money spells performed daily than any other sort of spell. Everybody wants love and money. But please, do not forget courage, wisdom, and even patience. These qualities can bring you all the sex and money you'll ever need. Remember to balance your magical activities and perform at least as many rituals to give you courage or wisdom as you do for sex and money.

Now let's examine the magical universe a little further.

Down to Earth Magic

𝔍 n order to do a successful operation in a any area of life, your subconscious must be completely filled with the symbols of that part of our magical universe. If you want to do a successful operation in the area of love, you will be working in the magical world of Netzach or Victory. This is the sphere of Venus, which is very appropriate. The correct color of this magical world is green. The appropriate scent would be Benzoin, Rose or Red Sandalwood.

If you want to perform a "love spell," you should arrange for your surroundings to be totally in tune with the world of Netzach and the spirit of Venus. Everything around you should remind you and re-program your subconscious to "think Venus". You would place seven candles around you, maybe even use green candles. You would wear emerald jewelry (if you have any) and burn red sandalwood incense. Maybe you have some rose oil and put a little of it on your forehead. You are now set to program your mind for love.

The magician would now proceed to either chant some invocations to impress on his mind what he wants to accomplish, or he might proceed to make and consecrate a talisman to draw to him what he desires. In a love spell we don't have to guess very hard what that might be.

As you can see, it is absolutely essential for any aspiring magician to understand the magical universe and its correspondences. Let them be a road map to where you wish to go. If you go to an occult bookstore, you can find many books that contain "spells" that you could use word for word. Believe me, anything that you can make up yourself, that comes from "the bottom of your heart," will work better than any pre-canned spell from a $4.95 K-mart spell book. As long as you prepare yourself and your surroundings properly, your magical workings will be successful.

When we discussed the magical worlds earlier, we learned the God names and the names of the angels and archangels. Naturally, they would be the ones we would direct our pleas to. Please learn all correspondences (the God-names, angels, colors, scents, etc.) They are essential for your magical work.

Talismans

A talisman or amulet is an object that has been given life or powers by means of a magical ceremony. Talismans are used for protection, bringing love or money, passing exams, and just about anything that can be classified within the ten magical worlds.

ou have probably heard the words talisman or amulet before. Most people think they are the same thing. Actually, a talisman is used to bring something to you, while an amulet keeps things away. You would make a talisman to bring you a thousand dollars and you would make an amulet to keep burglars out of your house. What is the actual difference between creating a talisman or an amulet?

A talisman is made during the period of an increasing (waxing) moon. An amulet is made during the decreasing (waning) moon. The moon is the celestial body closest to our own planet, and our lives are very closely connected to it. The length of the month is connected to the phases of the moon. The moon announces night time to us and even affects the tides. What better symbolism could you think of than connecting the making of a talisman or amulet to the decrease or increase of the moon?

How do we get a talisman? We could send for one of these "good luck charms" and pentagrams you'll find advertised in occult magazines, and sometimes even in the "National Enquirer. Remember what I said earlier, "A talisman is an object that has been given life or powers by means of a magical ceremony." How many ceremonies do you think the miracle charm manufacturer in Taiwan conducts to empower his mail-order talismans? None would be a good guess.

The power lies not in the object itself but in the fact that you make it mean something to your subconscious. It is essential that a talisman, or amulet is consecrated. On the other hand, the talisman itself should also have a connection with the proper magical world it is supposed to be operating in. A Netzach (Venus) talisman should have certain colors, numbers and names on it so it can properly represent the powers you want it to possess.

Let's try to construct a simple "love talisman." We could use a semi-precious stone or a piece of metal or wood, or we could simply use a piece of paper and write the appropriate magical signs or names on it. I know that does not sound very "magical." If you like to be a little more traditional, you might want to use a nice green stone, or at least some parchment type paper. Check the newspaper and make sure that the moon is on the increase. Now you are ready to put the appropriate signs and names on our talisman.

First of all, make up a figure that in your own mind most clearly represents what you are trying to achieve with this talisman. Do not put down a heart; that's too simple. Put down something that would be meaningless to anyone but you. Your own secret sign. This will be the most powerful sign you can use on any talisman. Since the color green is the appropriate color for the world of Netzach, we might want to use a green pen to write with. The next step would be to write on this piece of paper or other material, soon to be our talisman, the appropriate names of the magical world, the associated planet, the angels and archangels.

The number seven would also be appropriate, and it would be nice if you would use a total of seven signs and names on your talisman or amulet. Again, the list of correspondences will give all the appropriate references for any talisman or amulet that you might want to make.

Finally, if you feel you have exhausted all possible references on your talisman, it is time to give it power. After all, at this moment we still don't have much more than a worthless piece of paper, metal, or stone in front of us. On the other hand, by making the talisman and pondering over the correspondences, you have already sent out many subliminal messages to your brain and started to program it to bring you what you trying to accomplish. The actual consecration of the talisman will bring this programming into your subconscious mind.

To consecrate a talisman, unfortunately, we have to complicate matters a little. If you read old magic books like *The Key of Solomon* or *The Magus*, you will find one thing that is consistent through all of them. The use of "magical hours." You just don't consecrate a talisman or amulet whenever you feel like it. You do it at the proper time.

The ancients believed that each day of the week had it's correspondence to the magical worlds, and the names of the week attest to that. After all, Sunday is named after the sun. Monday after the moon and the rest of the days after Germanic Gods that also have their fixed place in our magical world.

Here again, we find a strong connection between our everyday world and the world of Magic. And you thought Monday was named just for the heck of it. No, there is Magic everywhere in our life. Magical hours are a sub-division of the magical days and the first hour after sunrise on a Monday would be the hour of the Moon. From thereon different planets rule the following hours of the day until the next day comes around. The system of magical hours is described in the Appendix to this book.

Unfortunately, it gets even more complicated. A magical hour is not always one hour long. A magical day starts at sunrise and ends at sundown. Then the magical night begins and continues until the next morning. We all know that winter nights are longer and summer nights are shorter. Here now comes the point in your life where you have to travel to your local supermarket and buy one of these famous "Farmer's Almanac" booklets you never knew what they were good for. These books, which only cost about two bucks, will tell you the exact times of sunrise and sunset.

Once you have determined when the sun rises and sets, you can then apply some simple math to divide your days and nights into accurate magical hours. Here is the way to do it. Take the total time between sunrise and sunset and divide by 12. This will be the length of your magical day hours.

By the same token, you can take the amount of hours between sunset and sunrise to calculate the magical night hours. Of course, you will find that in the winter, your magical night hours are longer than one actual hour and your magical days are shorter. The same is true in reverse during the summer.

Let's assume you want to consecrate your talisman at night. This is always a good idea because candle light during the daytime just doesn't get you in the right magical mood. More than likely there are much more disturbances during the daytime as well. Here is another mystery solved. Magicians do not work at night because they work "evil."

They work at night because there is less noise and a better atmosphere for the burning of candles. Now we need to find the proper hour in which to consecrate the talisman. If we make a "love" talisman, Friday is our magical day, and of course the first hour of the "magical night" would be the proper hour to do our ritual in. That way we have the power of the proper day and hour going for us. We could also use another day to do our consecration as long as we do it during the proper hour. Let's say we want to do a consecration on a Tuesday. A quick scan of our table will tell us that the fifth hour is the hour of Venus on that particular day.

If, for example, sunset is at 5;00 p.m., and our magical hour is one hour and 10 minutes long that means that the proper time for the ritual is between 10:50 and 12:00. I know that was a lot of calculating but then, you probably don't have to consecrate talismans more than once a month.

A talisman should keep its power during the entire month, until the next full moon. It can always be re-consecrated, or you can burn it and make a new one next time around and consecrate that one when the time is right. Remember to burn or bury your talisman when it has served its time. You want the powers you instilled in it to dissipate peacefully. A talisman that is still active and is just left lying around is a disaster waiting to happen. The fact that you carelessly discard a magical object indicates that you obviously do not believe in its powers very much.

All that's left for you to do now is to consecrate the talisman. Here are some suggestions on how to do this. You can of course make up your own "incantation" but you should follow these basic guidelines. Prepare yourself for the ritual by taking a leisurely bath, then put on your magical robe and step in front of your altar (or table, or whatever you use to put your candles on.) We already described some of the attributes that should be present to put yourself in that "Venus mood" and we assume you have taken care of all that. Let us also assume that your talisman is lying on the altar, ready to be consecrated.

Make sure you have everything you need for your magical operation within reach. You have no idea how easy it is to forget something, even something as important as the talisman in question that you left lying somewhere on the kitchen table. Of course, every magician knows that, once you began an operation, you should under no circumstances step out of the circle. Again, this is not because some evil spirits are going to get you but rather because when you come back out of the kitchen the magical atmosphere you tried to create has probably long gone. After all, that's what it is all about. So you are standing in front of your altar in your magical clothing. You have lighted your candles and your incense. Maybe you are playing a little soft new age music in the background. You are ready!

First, try to relax as much as you can and concentrate on the atmosphere of Venus that you have created. You are no longer in your bedroom or living room; you are in the magical world of Venus. You can almost see Aphrodite and some other Greek Goddesses before you. If they look really sexy to you and you get turned on, that's not too bad either. At least you know something is happening. Now do the Lesser Banishing Ritual of the Pentagram. We discussed it earlier and by now you should be doing it regularly and should be pretty confident with it. The LBRP is the basis of all our magical workings and you really shouldn't even attempt to consecrate a talisman if you haven't done your LBRP's for at least a month.

Patience is the key to magical success. You can work a certain operation for years, gaining a minuscule bit more every time you do it, and suddenly, maybe after a year, you realize how powerful you have become. Change in Magic is slow but sure.

By doing the LBRP, you have created a magical circle around you. You have also protected yourself from all negative influences that might surround you, or are occupying your mind for that matter. You are ready to consecrate your talisman.

Concentrate on the cross of light that you have created inside yourself when you started the LBRP, and try to mentally intensify this light. Picture yourself surrounded by this bright white light. Feel it pulsating and gaining strength. Make this cross of light inside your body as bright as you can. Now change the color of the light to the color of the magical world you are working in. In this case, change your color to a bright emerald green. Now pick up the talisman with your right hand. Now see and feel the green light being drawn into the talisman. Now say, "I invoke the archangel Haniel. Charge and consecrate this talisman" Then call on the choir of angels and say, "I invoke the Elohim. Charge and consecrate this talisman."

Finally say, "By the power of Yod-He-Vau-He Tzavaoth, charge and consecrate this talisman." This is the appropriate God name. While you do this, feel the green light and the power in yourself increasing. Feel it glow and come to life. Now say aloud the purpose of the talisman.

Feel all the green light rush into the talisman, then put it down and say, "So mote it be." This means, you have done what you have set out to do and there is no doubt in your mind that it will work. You have stated that you are a magician, and if you do your Magic, invariably, you'll see results.

Now put your talisman away into whatever container you want to keep it in. If you want to keep it on your person, a little bag would be perfect. Of course, you might have consecrated an amulet to keep burglars (or your mother in law) out of your house. In that case, you would place this amulet near the door where it can scare the stuffing out of any burglar. Keep your amulets or talismans where they are needed to do their stuff. You would keep your love talisman near your heart and your anti-car-accident amulet on the dashboard. It is always a good idea not to let anyone touch it. The idea of profane hands touching it might not sit very good with your subconscious.

I gave you an example of a love talisman consecration. To consecrate a talisman or amulet for any other purpose requires nothing but a substitution of the correspondences. A money talisman would need Jupiter attributes like the number four and the color blue, and for it's consecration you would call on a different set of angels and use a different God name.

et me clear something up about these God names. Some people get upset and say, "There is only one God. What you are doing is worshipping false Gods or idols." But then, I did not say you were to call on different Gods, just use different God names. Just like a store clerk would call you "Sir" while your wife or husband calls you "Sugar," or sometimes "Jerk" and your boss usually calls you by your last name, they are still all calling the same person.

The type of name you call someone really gives them a hint to your relationship with them. You wouldn't call your boss "Sugar" and your wife "Madam." Here again, we find our correspondences. You will call on different qualities of whatever God you believe in, whether we ask him for financial favors or we ask him to send us a beautiful lover to have and to hold.

The Secrets of the Tarot

arot cards and Magic are invariably linked together. The Tarot goes back as far as ancient Egypt, where most Magic originated. The Tarot cards correspond perfectly with our magical universe. Every card in the deck relates directly to one of the 10 magical worlds or a connecting path between two worlds.

This is a book about Magic, not the Tarot, so I can't give you a complete description of all the cards in this book. What I want to discuss here is what the Tarot can do for you. If you are interested in the meanings of the Tarot cards and their correspondences to the magical worlds, I recommend my book *Down to Earth Tarot*. This book is available at your local bookstore or directly from ABACO Publishing.

A magician will use the Tarot cards to probe his subconscious for answers to questions that his conscious mind is unable to answer. If you do a Tarot reading to find out if you'll ever find your perfect match and get married, a reading can help you find the answers. There is no supernatural power that will manipulate the cards and tell you the future. On the contrary, it's your subconscious response, or what you are reading "into" the cards, that will reveal the potentials for a particular situation.

If the cards are telling you that you will not find a compatible mate it might be that subconsciously you have been rejecting potential partners because of some hang-up. The Tarot cards might reveal to you the nature of your hang-ups so you can do something about it. And this is the true power of the Tarot.

Tarot cards are the gateway to your subconscious, your hidden feelings and hang-ups. You are reading the Tarot cards with the expectation of finding something hidden and unknown. That's why your conscious mind will not interfere too much with your interpretation. The subconscious can send its message through unhindered. So there it is. The secret of the Tarot. Do not pay too much attention to the exact meaning of the cards but concentrate on your subconscious reactions. What you read into the cards is what's really important.

What practical uses are there for the Tarot? You might want to do a Tarot card reading before undertaking anything you are not sure of. The cards will tell you whether you can pull it off or not. Deep inside you'll know whether you can handle it or not. It is always a good idea to get some insight from your subconscious before doing any magical operation, especially a spell, talisman consecration or exorcism. You might think the operation is a good idea, but your subconscious might know better. Very often, a Tarot card reading will reveal some things you might have overlooked. Based on your reading you can then make a final decision on whether to do a magical operation or not. You should definitely do a Tarot card reading before doing an exorcism. Your subconscious will tell you whether it is wise to ostracize a particular part of your personality or not.

Another great use for these cards is in your "Easy Magic" ESP training. Sure, a deck of playing cards will work, but the intricate meanings and messages hidden in the Tarot will work better in activating your mind than plain numbers and symbols. Some very wise men spent years and years developing the Tarot and it has been proven to work for centuries. Try the ESP training exercise from the "Easy Magic" chapter in this book with a deck of Tarot cards. Then look up the meanings of the cards. See how often you have picked a card that is very close in meaning to the actual card on the table. This is what you want to achieve with your ESP training exercise. You want to train your mind to pick up concepts and feelings rather than exact numbers, colors and symbols.

If I made you curious and you would like to purchase a Tarot deck, I recommend the Rider-Waite deck. It is the most used and easiest to interpret. If you really want to get an exotic deck with deep hidden meanings, you might want to check out Aleister Crowley's Thoth deck. Both decks mentioned are available in most bookstores. If your store doesn't carry Tarot decks you can order them directly from ABACO Publishing.

If you would like to read up more on the subject of Tarot, learn how to do different spreads and how to interpret cards, you might want to look into my book *Down to Earth Tarot*. It contains very complete descriptions of all 78 cards, and several different ways to spread the cards. There is a lot of no nonsense advice on how to get meaningful and reliable Tarot readings in the pages of *Down to Earth Tarot*.

More about energy

his chapter is about elemental energy. About the powers of Fire, Air, Earth, and Water. There are a lot of things in Magic that you should not take literally. After all, Magic uses the language of symbolism. The elements are a good example of that.

When a magician works with the powers of Fire, he doesn't actually conjure up fires, or work with some mysterious spiritual force that looks and acts like fire. He uses his personal "Fire." Fire is enthusiasm, courage, daring, swiftness.

You could probably come up with a lot of human qualities that correspond to certain elements. Earth is dependability, responsibility, being "money-wise" or simply "down to earth." Water would be sensitivity, compassion, forgiveness, spirituality, and others. Air represents thinking that is very lofty or idealistic.

The ultimate goal of any magician should be to have all these energies perfectly balanced in him. In practice, most people will lack in one or the other department. An "airhead" is somebody who is generally not very "down to earth" and may not be very good in handeling money matters. He is desperately in need of some earthly qualities, while a very "fiery" pushy and cold hearted business man might need some lessons in spirituality and compassion. He would need some "watery" qualities in his life. Since Magic is all about symbolism, I really don't see any problems in using the names "Earth, Fire, Air, and Water" to represent areas of our psyche.

If you perform a ceremony that involves the sphere of Earth, and the appropriate magical world that goes with it, you will balance your personality a little more in that direction. Remember when you consecrated the talisman? You used the light you had "conjured up" inside your body to charge the talisman with. Next time you want a charge of a certain energy, try changing that light-energy you built up with the LBRP ritual into "Earth" or "Fire." See and feel it change color and texture. Let it engulf you with its energy.

If you need more "Fire" in your life, change your energy to "Fire." Feel the heat. See the light inside you change color and turn red and orange like a flame. You can also let off energy like that. If you are lazy and have too much "Earth" in you, try to work up that Earth energy inside you. Instead of leaving it inside you, imagine it flowing out of your body the same way it did when we charged that talisman. Only this time, let it flow out in front of you and then simply go "pouff." You have just released energy of which you simply had too much.

Another way to use energy is to create an "elemental life form." An elemental life form does what a talisman or amulet does, only it is not an existing physical thing but an "artificial creature" created by the power of your mind and energized with the energy of a certain element.

Will such a non-existing creature be as effective as a "real life" talisman? Remember what you learned in the first chapter in this book. Anything you create in your mind is as effective as something you actually experience in "real life." Let's say created an "elemental life-form" made out of Earth to help you with overspending, and to help you be more responsible with your money. I'll bet the next time when you pull out a credit card for that sweater that you really don't need, your little "elemental life form" will pop up in your head to tell you, "Don't do it."

How then do you create such an "elemental?" Well, you proceed very much like you do when you charge a talisman. You do not have to wait for any particular hour or day to do it, but you should have your surroundings arranged so they correspond with the particular world, and element, you are working with.

Let's say we want to create an "elemental" to bring us money. We would create it out of Earth, since we want some very material and "down to earth" things from it. The appropriate sphere would, of course, be that of Jupiter. The number would be 4 and the color would be blue.

Start out just like with any other magical working, with the Lesser Banishing Ritual of the Pentagram. This will clear the air from all negativity and make you feel more like a "real magician." After you've finished the LBRP, just as in the talisman consecration, concentrate on the light inside yourself and turn it into Earth energy. You will feel a solidity but also warmth and comfort. The light will turn green or brown and you feel nature and growth inside you. Now raise your right arm up straight in front of you and point to the area right behind your altar (but still inside your circle.)

Let the energy flow out toward this point and start to concentrate there. Let the Earth energy take on the shape you would want your elemental life form to have. This could be absolutely anything. It could be a certain animal or simply a cloud or a ball of energy.

When you feel all the elemental energy has left your body and is inside your elemental, keep pointing at it and say with a firm voice, "I hereby name thee _____." Give it any name you like, but make sure it is appropriate to it's purpose. Go and do such and such. Name the thing you want it to do. But remember to tell it only ONE THING that it should do.

The poor thing is made up out of only one element, so it surely can't accomplish dozens of different things that you couldn't even do yourself. Since you are creating an elemental with the purpose to get more money, you might say, "I hereby call you GRAB-EM. I want you to go and find new customers for my business, grab them and bring them to me." You will probably find new customers coming out of the woodwork real soon.

Remember, you get out of it what you put into it. Always give it all you've got when you work up the energy to create the elemental. After all, it's you, the magician that makes it happen. You will also find that elementals have the tendency to "fizzle out" rather fast, especially if you didn't put very much energy into making them. You can always call an elemental back to a ceremony and re-charge it, or you could create a new one. It is very important to understand that if you "discard" an elemental, you have to absorb him back into your body. Once you feel your elemental has done its job or one month has gone by, call him back during one of your daily banishings. Make sure you see him clearly before you, then let him become one with you again.

Elementals can take up some kind of "life of their own" and actually wreak some havoc. The infamous "poltergeist" phenomena is a good example of human energy let loose without a purpose. Nobody has an explanation yet of how "Poltergeist" come into being, but too many people have witnessed them first hand to deny that this phenomena exists. Your energy can take on very "real" forms, on the other hand, the practice of making artificial elementals can be very rewarding.

Making things go away

$\mathcal{S}$ometimes you don't want to create anything or receive anything, but you have a bad character trait that you want to get rid off. You might not be assertive enough to get the promotion you deserve, and you would like to get rid of your timidness. If any of this rings a bell, it might be time for you to play the "Exorcist."

here are dozens of books in the archives of the Vatican that deal with exorcisms. In the middle ages, exorcisms were very common. Anybody who in some way acted abnormal, depressed, or somehow unusual, was assumed to be possessed by some kind of demon. In today's enlightened age we have more straightforward explanations for "strange" behavior. You might have psychological problems. You might be extremely shy or depressed, act very hostile, or something similar. Usually in such cases we call in today's exorcists. We find them in the Yellow Pages under the heading of "Psychiatrists."

Now why is it that modern day psychiatrists have so much trouble pinpointing what's wrong with somebody? Why do people that go to therapy spend years there? Well, you guessed it. Psychiatrists do not practice Magic. They try to probe into a person's psyche with scientific methods, come up with all kinds of syndroms and complexes, and only rarely seem to accomplish something concrete.

A magician's philosophy is different. He does not care whether you have an aggrevated rejection complex, you secretly hate your father, or you've been beaten up by your sister once too often. All a magician cares about is that there is something wrong with your mind. And whatever it is, it has to go. It's that simple.

In good old-fashioned exorcists terms, you are plagued by a demon of some kind. If you can kill the demon, or at least ask him to leave you alone from now on, you'll be cured. A a demon is something we can easily picture in our mind, and we can also picture us destroying this demon.

How do you picture an aggrevated rejection complex in your mind? This is the problem with conventional methods. Psychologists and psychiatrists work with such abstract concepts and terms. It's hard to deal with them on an every day person's level. That's why exorcisms work. If you can picture your troubles as a demon, you can deal with a it. Remember, anything you can do in your mind can come true in real life.

How does a magician get rid of his problems? First, he identifies the problem. Let me give you a simple example. Say you have been passed over for promotions too many times; your love life isn't quite what it could be either. The reason? You're just too shy to get what you want out of life. Many people have this problem and it is something anybody can easily relate to. Yet, it is incredibly hard to cure shyness. You can spend years in therapy and still not come out much better in the end. So, you have identified your problem. Shyness!

The next thing a magical approach calls for is to give this problem a shape and form, so you can deal with it. After all, shyness is the demon you are trying to exorcise, so let's picture him in your mind as a demon.

Give him a name. Not shyness; that's too simple. Let's call him DRAG-EN, since he has been dragging you down and holding you back for years.

Picture him in your mind as vividly as you can. What color is he? How tall? How many feet and hands? You might want to give him eight hands since he always did a pretty good job of holding you back. Now that you have given him a name and know what he looks like, picture him in your mind every day for about two weeks. You want him to become very real to you.

After two weeks it's time for your exorcism ritual. Make all the usual preparations you would do for any other ceremony. You don't have to worry about planetary hours or colors or any other correspondences. You are doing a banishing. Only this time it's not a general banishing. You are banishing a specific demon. Naturally, you are starting out with the Banishing Ritual of the Pentagram to clear the air, get you in the right mood and, most of all, to build a nice strong circle around you.

Here comes the dangerous part. The circle usually protects the magician from any bad influence around him, so it is very important that this circle is in good shape. After all, you are practicing Magic, and you are stirring a lot of things up in the spirit world (your mind.) Something could be attracted by all of that hoopla and decide to do you harm. The circle will prevent this from happening.

In this particular ceremony we are dealing with something that is inside you, your personal demon. When it is time to battle him, he will be INSIDE your circle and you will try to get him out where he can't do any more harm to you. When I mentioned this as being the dangerous part, it's because you need to be a more seasoned magician to battle a demon inside the circle. Even though nothing will physically attack you, I recommend that you only do this kind of ritual when you feel in top shape and are very sure about your status as an accomplished magician.

Now let's get back to your ceremony. After you are finished with the banishing ritual, you will start picturing the demon in front of you, inside the circle. You'll see his energy slowly leaving your body and accumulating in his. Remember, this is only HIS energy. Do not give him any of your own. As you have him clearly standing in front of you, we call him by his name and really let him have it. Tell him you're not going to take it anymore, that he will have to leave, and that his tyranny is now over.

Now lift up your finger and draw a bright pentagram in front of him. This pentagram is just like the ones in the banishing, but it should be inside the circle between you and your troubles (demon.) Now muster all of your energy and say, "DRAG-EN be gone!" While doing this push the pentagram outward until it is outside the circle. The pentagram will push your demon out with it and the demon is now outside the circle.

Lift up your finger again and send some more energy out to him so you will slowly zap him. See him disintegrate and eventually completely disappear. Now quickly do your banishing ritual again. After all, you just punched a hole in your circle and you want to mend this hole as quickly as possible. This ritual can be repeated as often as necessary and you will find that your demon will get weaker every time. Very often, the first time is all that's needed.

Another warning is in order here. Be careful about what you are exorcising. For example, if you are exorcising your shyness, realize that this shyness might be a very integral part of your personality. You might find that you successfully exorcised your shyness, but suddenly find yourself becoming hard and cold. Any part of your personality is a part of you and it has its good and bad sides. Sometimes it is better to be shy and a generally nice person rather than being hard and cold.

Be sure to contemplate very carefully what you are doing, and be careful what you wish for. You might get it. Remember, this is an important point in Magic. Specify very clearly what you want to achieve with your magical operation. Never generalize. You'll end up like the guy who found a Genie in a bottle that granted him three wishes. He ended up using up his last wish just to undo the first two.

In Magic, you always get exactly what you wish for. If you create a talisman to get "a woman," you might end up with the ugliest woman that ever lived. If you specify "a beautiful woman," you might end up with a beautiful calculating gold digger. Be careful about what you wish for. Being a magician, you will usually get it.

More Easy Magic

he key to success in Magic is the training of the mind. In the "Easy Magic" chapter you've learned to train and test your intuition and ESP potential. Here are some more great tricks and exercises for your mind.

TRAINING YOUR INNER CLOCK

This exercise will help in attuning yourself to nature and your inner clock. Almost everybody has an alarm clock in their house. It prevents you from oversleeping and makes sure you're not late for work or school. But a real magician doesn't really need an alarm clock. Actually, he doesn't even need a watch. Living by the clock every day of your life, you should already have the flow of time well ingrained in your mind. Unfortunately, since you always look at that stupid watch to find out what time it is, your inner clock has moved from your conscious mind to a 2 Bedroom Condo in the subconscious. And both bedrooms have a "Do not disturb" sign on the door. Let's get that inner clock working again, so you will always know what time it is. And you will never have to set your alarm again.

Here is a simple exercise that puts you back in good standing with your inner clock. The next time you want to wake up at a certain time, don't set your alarm. Go to bed and relax. Breathe deeply and empty your mind of all the problems and worries of the day. Now concentrate on the time you want to get up. Picture the face your clock in front of you, showing exactly the time you want to get up. See waking up in the morning. Make this as real as you can. Then relax again and go to sleep, knowing that you will wake up at the exact time you need to wake up.

But don't be overanxious about this. If you are, you'll possibly wake up long before its really time for you to get up. Your mind is so anxious that it will make sure you wake up real early.

Once your inner alarm clock is working well for you, you can start working on your inner wrist watch, so you always know what time it is. I know it's not really a big deal to look at your watch, but try leaving it at home one day. You feel as helpless as a child. You'll ask people for the time every 2 minutes and you feel genuinely handicapped. Let's train that inner clock, so we never feel helpless again.

Here is a simple exercise to get your inner clock on track again. Every time you go to bed, turn out the light so you can't see the time on your alarm clock. If you have one with lighted dials, just don't look. Visualize your alarm clock in front of you. See it with your mind's eye. See the position of the big and small hand and read the time off this clock in your mind. Don't check with your actual clock whether you're right or wrong for at least a few days. Just visualize the clock, look at the time, and forget it. Please don't use your reasoning powers to figure out what time it SHOULD BE. Don't say to yourself, "I watched the eleven o' clock news, then brushed my teeth and went to bed, so it must be about 11:10PM." You do not want to access your conscious clock; you want the one in your subconscious, the clock that is never wrong and never needs winding. So just see the clock. Do not argue or reason with it.

After a few days you can check with your real clock and see how accurate you've been. Continue this exercise until you are always on the mark. Of course you can also do this exercise while you are out somewhere. Leave your watch at home sometime and use your inner clock. The more you use it, the more reliable it becomes. Sooner or later, you won't need your wrist watch at all. You have successfully fixed your inner clock. This exercise will greatly enhance your access to the subconscious and will make any other exercise in this book more effective, too.

A TUNE-UP FOR YOUR BRAIN

Stress is a problem for all of us, and we all wish there was a simple and effective cure-all solution. Well, there is! This particular "Easy Magic Trick" is the only one in this book that requires a little help from modern technology. And why not? Just because you are practicing Magic, doesn't mean you have to live in the stone age and forsake all modern comforts. But let's get back to reducing stress.

What happens when you are under pressure? Your brain switches into high gear and your brainwave frequency goes up. The opposite will take place when you relax or sleep. The more you relax, the more your brainwaves will slow down.

Many studies have been done to explore the different levels of brain activity a person can achieve. Generally speaking, a wide awake person will have brainwaves of about 100 cycles per minute. A person under stress can easily push this up to 160 and more. On the other hand, a person on the threshold of sleep will find his brain slow down to about 60 to 80 cycles per minute. A person that's totally relaxed or under hypnosis (which is also a very relaxed state), will also have this low brainwave activity.

Scientists call this state of low brainwave activity the "Alpha" state. Whenever you are in "Alpha," a lot of amazing things will happen to you. The "Alpha" state is not only a state of relaxation, it is also a state of high mental activity. Memory retention is three to four times as high as under normal conditions. This means, if you study while in "Alpha," you will remember up to four times as much when you're finished. Another miracle of "Alpha" is that you are much more open to intuition and inspiration. "Alpha" is a true state of miracles. After all, that's what a magician is after. Every magical operation done in the "Alpha" state will be much more powerful and effective. Relieving stress, increasing your memory, and increasing your intuition? That almost sounds too good to be true. Yet, it's quite easy to achieve this state.

Let us first look at some traditional ways to achieve "Alpha." You are this state just after falling asleep and just before waking up. This is the time when you dream heavily. The only dreams you can remember after you wake up are dreams experienced in the "Alpha" state.

This confirms the high mental activity that happens in the "Alpha" state. Unfortunately, going to sleep is rarely a solution for job stress, and studying while sleeping doesn't work either. So, the natural "Alpha" state is of no good for our purposes.

Another way to achieve "Alpha" is under hypnosis. Under hypnosis, you are extremely relaxed and on the other hand very mentally alert. A lot of hypnotists are using a watch or some kind of pendulum. They swing it in front of the patients eyes at, of course, about 60 swings per minute. There is this magical figure again. The person to be hypnotized will concentrate on the pendulum and the brain will lock in on that magic rhythm of 60 cycles per minute.

More technology minded hypnotists are using a machine called the brainwave synchronizer to get their patients into the "Alpha" state. The brainwave synchronizer is basically a strobe light that flickers on and off at, you guessed it, about 60 flashes per minute.

In Europe, a lot of traffic accidents happend on country roads that had trees planted in regular intervals. Once the automobilist reached a certain speed, the reflected light from the headlights hit the unsuspecting driver at exactly 60 cycles per minute. This put the drivers into the "Alpha" state. If they were already sleepy, it caused them to fall asleep and crash into the trees. Somebody real clever discovered what happend to these drivers and used the same principles to invent the brainwave synchronizer.

Unfortunately, a brainwave synchronizer is not very affordable. The flashing lights wouldn't really allow you to study while using it either. Something else is needed to achieve the "Alpha" state.

After studying all these facts, I found the solution. Why not use sound instead of light? Sound will not interfere with any studying or reading you might want to do. You can even use it when you are too stressed out to help you fall asleep. A lot of hypnotists use a metronome for relaxation purposes. It's relatively inexpensive and it is very easy to set it to 60 cycles per minute. A still less expensive method is to borrow a metronome, put a tape recorder in front of it and record the sound for later use.

A tape with the magical clicking sound of 60 cycles per minute will help you relax or fall asleep when you have troubles sleeping. It can even help you retain more when you study. Of course, you can also play the tape in the background while doing any magical operation. This will help you relax and concentrate on the operation at hand.

If you don't want to go through the hassles of making your own tapes, you can order them from the store that you purchased this book from or directly from ABACO Publishing. Their address is in the back of this book. The tapes are called "Psychotronics Tapes" and they sell for $9.95 a piece. These tapes are actually a little more effective than the ones you can make yourself. Psychotronics tapes are not clicking at a constant speed but they start at a high speed and then gradually change to the low "Alpha" freqeuency.

This will help your brain "lock in" on the right frequency regardless of your level of stress and then slow it down gradually. There is even a "Psychotronics" sleep tape available that doesn't stop at 60 cycles per minute but takes you all the way down to 40 cycles per minute. This is called "Theta" or deep sleep.

The "Alpha" state is truly a magical condition. Try it, you'll like it.

More about the White Light

When you do a Banishing Ritual or Self-Hypnosis Session, you will picture yourself engulfed by a white light. Actually, most magical operations use this white light.

I bet by now, you are very curious to find out more about this mysterious light.

By conjuring up the white light in your mind, you are giving your human energy a visible form. As mentioned in many chapters before, a magician can't work with anything he can't make visible in his mind. What you can picture in your mind, you can make happen in real life. This white light is the magician's energy, his secret power. By making this energy visible, he can direct it to wherever it is needed.

A good example of using this white light is healing. Any good magician can help a friend or lover's headache disappear in a flash. Headaches are usually caused by the mind to start with. Something upsets you or worries you. That's the real cause of the headache. Very rarely will a headache be caused by something purely physical. And when you think about it, a lot of illness and disease is caused, at least partially, by the mind. When a magician heals somebody, he uses his mind to accomplish this feat.

The results you'll achieve depend on your own energy levels. If you are weak, worried, or ill, you can't heal anybody. It is important, before you attempt to heal someone, to re-charge your own batteries and get your energy levels up. There is no better way to do this than the Lesser Banishing Ritual of the Pentagram. This ceremony literally bathes you in the white light. If you do the LBRP every day, your energy levels will increase tremendously.

If you just need a quick boost, you can do this: Sit down in a comfortable chair and make sure you are not disturbed. Relax yourself. Breathe slowly and deeply. Picture the white light entering your body at the top of your head and slowly spreading all over your body. Let yourself be engulfed by the light for about two minutes. Now you are finished. When leaving your chair, do not picture the white light to disappear, but keep in mind that this light is there to stay long after you've finished.

Now you are ready to heal. Headaches are the easiest to get rid of, and you'll have the most success with loved ones or friends. Let's assume you want to relieve your mate's headache. Put your left hand just left of the center of the pain and your right hand to the right. Picture the pain as a car battery that you've just connected jumper cables to. Now concentrate on the light energy inside you. Make it visible in your mind's eye again. Feel it slowly moving down your right hand into your mate's body, cleansing and flushing out the pain. Now feel the energy flow back into your left hand and up into your own body. All the mental junk is flushed out by this stream of energy and caught up in the white light.

Here is one word of warning. Not only do you bring healthy, healing energy into your mate's body, you also flush some sickness and pain back out into your own body to be absorbed. That's why it is so important that your energy levels are high.

If you take in more than you can safely absorb, you might start feeling a little sick yourself. Don't let that keep you from helping your mate or friend. If you are healthy and full of energy, you can easily absorb their pain.

Continue the flow of energy until you feel that the area you are working on is flushed out well and pulsating with the vibrant white light energy. Your mate's headache will be gone, or at least considerably less. The more you practice this, the more effective your healing powers will become. Don't be disappointed if you are not too successful the first time around.

When you are healing someone, by all means, explain to them exactly what you are doing. Tell them about the energy you are sending them, and the flushing out of pain and disease. If they understand what you are doing, their mind can help work on the healing process.

You might have read about some psychic healers who have cured many, some even famous people. These healers have an extraordinary amount of human energy and are indeed very effective. I won't say that you will ever become a natural healer, but being a magician and doing your LBRP's regularly will increase your energy levels enormously. Relieving your mate's headaches and stress should be a snap for you.

Another way you can use the white light is for protection. The Banishing Ritual of the Pentagram is a good example. It builds a protective barrier around you and keeps you from harm and negative influences. Every time you do the LBRP a little more of the white light energy will permanently stay with you. I assume, after doing the LBRP for a few years, to a psychic sensitive person you must look like a christmas tree.

It is good to know that the white light is there to protect you from harm. Then again, there is no reason why this light couldn't be used to protect other persons and things as well. The next time you are going on a trip, try to extend the white light energy all the way around your house.

No evil doer or burglar would dare go near a house that he feels subconsciously, is so brightly lit. The would be burglar will not actually see any physical light around your house, but something will tell him that it might not be a good idea to burglarize this house.

The same principle will also work for your other belongings. Your car is a good example. A little white light each day will keep the body shop away. Now there's a cheap insurance policy. I can see the bumper sticker now: Insured by White Light Insurance.

Another great side effect of the white light is that it, pardon the pun, puts you in a better light when interacting with other people. Customers will trust you more readily. Friends will like you better. Even the opposite sex will find you more attractive.

You don't believe it? Well, I'll give you something to think about. The next time you walk into a crowded room, look at the strangers around you. Some people you can easily imagine yourself being friends with, others you dislike almost instantly. This is really not a physical thing and what these people look like has nothing to do with it. Some people you like immediately, others you immediately dislike. I am not saying that the people you like instantly are all practicing Magic and, so to speak, "have their lights on", but some people just radiate a lot of positive energy. This is the same energy you are calling on when you create and intensify the white light.

The next time you are standing next to a person you'd really like to meet, picture the white light energy coming down into your head just as described earlier on in this chapter. Then watch out for a positive reaction from this person. It's hard to ignore somebody that is bathed in positive energy.

You are welcome to experiment with the white light as much as you want. It's like silly putty. You can do anything with it. Try making it stronger and stronger inside you. It works wonders.

Some final thoughts

Practicing Magic can be very rewarding. Not only do you accomplish more in life, you usually become a happier, more balanced person. I have set out to write down in simple terms, without getting heavily into metaphysics, what Magic is all about. I hope I succeeded in that.

There are hundreds of books about Magic out there. Most of them are not really easy to understand. I hope this book will give you enough knowledge to continue your studies in Magic successfully. Books by Aleister Crowley and other members of the Golden Dawn will give you plenty of interesting material to study. If you would like to contact me for any comments or questions about this book, wish to order more copies of this book, or hire me for a speaking engagement or seminar, please write to:

Alan Steward
c/o ABACO Publishing Co., Inc.
P.O. Box 190094 Birmingham,
AL 35219
U.S.A.
or call (800) 685-4287
FAX (205) 833-4300

Appendix

Charts of Planetary Hours and Correspondences

Magical Hours after Sunrise

Sunrise	Sunday	Monday	Tuesday	Wednesday	Thursday	Friday	Saturday
1st Hour	Sun	Moon	Mars	Mercury	Jupiter	Venus	Saturn
2nd Hour	Venus	Saturn	Sun	Moon	Mars	Mercury	Jupiter
3rd Hour	Mercury	Jupiter	Venus	Saturn	Sun	Moon	Mars
4th Hour	Moon	Mars	Mercury	Jupiter	Venus	Saturn	Sun
5th Hour	Saturn	Sun	Moon	Mars	Mercury	Jupiter	Venus
6th Hour	Jupiter	Venus	Saturn	Sun	Moon	Mars	Mercury
7th Hour	Mars	Mercury	Jupiter	Venus	Saturn	Sun	Moon
8th Hour	Sun	Moon	Mars	Mercury	Jupiter	Venus	Saturn
9th Hour	Venus	Saturn	Sun	Moon	Mars	Mercury	Jupiter
10th Hour	Mercury	Jupiter	Venus	Saturn	Sun	Moon	Mars
11th Hour	Moon	Mars	Mercury	Jupiter	Venus	Saturn	Sun
12th Hour	Saturn	Sun	Moon	Mars	Mercury	Jupiter	Venus

Magical Hours after Sunset

Sunset	Sunday	Monday	Tuesday	Wednesday	Thursday	Friday	Saturday
1st Hour	Jupiter	Venus	Saturn	Sun	Moon	Mars	Mercury
2nd Hour	Mars	Mercury	Jupiter	Venus	Saturn	Sun	Moon
3rd Hour	Sun	Moon	Mars	Mercury	Jupiter	Venus	Saturn
4th Hour	Venus	Saturn	Sun	Moon	Mars	Mercury	Jupiter
5th Hour	Mercury	Jupiter	Venus	Saturn	Sun	Moon	Mars
6th Hour	Moon	Mars	Mercury	Jupiter	Venus	Saturn	Sun
7th Hour	Saturn	Sun	Moon	Mars	Mercury	Jupiter	Venus
8th Hour	Jupiter	Venus	Saturn	Sun	Moon	Mars	Mercury
9th Hour	Mars	Mercury	Jupiter	Venus	Saturn	Sun	Moon
10th Hour	Sun	Moon	Mars	Mercury	Jupiter	Venus	Saturn
11th Hour	Venus	Saturn	Sun	Moon	Mars	Mercury	Jupiter

Magical World	Color	Scent/Incense	Planets
Kether	White	Ambergris	The Universe
Hochma	Gray	Musk	The Zodiac
Binah	Black	Myrrh	Saturn
Hesed	Blue	Cedar	Jupiter
Geburah	Scarlet Red	Tobacco	Mars
Tipharet	Gold	Olibanum	The Sun
Netzach	Green	Rose	Venus
Hode	Orange	Storax	Mercury
Yesode	Violet	Jasmine	The Moon
Malkuth	Brown, Black	Dittany of Crete	The 4 Elements

Tables of Correspondences

Magical World	God Name	Arch Angel	Angels
Kether	Eh-Heh-Yeh	Metatron	Chai-oht Kahdesh
Hochma	Yah	Ratziel	Auphanim
Binah	Yehovauh Elohim	Tzaphkiel	Aralim
Hesed	El	Tzadkiel	Chasmalim
Geburah	Elohim Gibor	Khamael	Seraphim
Tipharet	Yehovauh Elohah Vadaath	Raphael	Amalachim
Netzach	Yehovauh Tzavaoth	Haniel	Elohim
Hode	Elohim Tzavaoth	Michael	Beney Elohim
Yesode	Shaddai El Chai	Gabriel	Kerubim
Malkuth	Adonai Melech	Sandalphon	Ashim

INDEX

A

Adam and Eve, 18
Additional Reading, 61
Air, 55 - 56,79, 82, 109 - 110
Airhead, 110
Aleister Crowley, *see*
  Crowley, Aleister
"Alpha" State, 127 - 130
Altar, 32,85, 98 - 99

Amulet, 29, 62, 73,91, 93 - 95,
101, 111
Ancient Books, 46, 56
Angels, 58 - 59, 61, 94, 100 - 101
Aphrodite, 99
Aralim, 60
Archangel(s), 58 - 59, 61,82 - 83,
94,100
Astral Plane, 58
Astrologers, 37
Astrological Signs, 57
Astrolog, 37
Atom(s), 37,38
Auphanim, 61
Auriel, 56,83
Autopilot, 20

B

Bad Programming, 11
Banishing, 75, 77, 81, 84 - 85,
113, 118
Banishing Ritual, 119 - 120, 131
Beauty, 59
Beney Elohim, 59
Benzoin, 89
Bible, the, 14, 18, 57
Binah, 56, 60 - 61
Black Magic, 40, 81
Books, Magic, 32
Brain, 9, 11, 19, 95

Brainwave Frequency, 126
Brainwaves, 126 - 127
Brainwave Synchronizer, 128 - 129
Breathing, 69
Brilliant Ones, 60
Business, 113

C

Candles, 32, 79, 89, 97, 99
Caribbean Vacation, 68
Catch, the, 21
Cedar, 60
Center of the Universe, 79
Ceremony, 73, 75, 79, 81, 93,
110, 113, 118 - 119
Charity, 65
Chasmalim, 60
Cherubim, 58
Chokmah, 56
Circle, magical, 99,112, 118 - 120
Clothes, magical, 31,30, 32
Coincidences, 71
Collective Consciousness, 52
Color, 32, 46, 53, 56, 58 - 62, 70,
72, 89, 94, 100, 110, 112, 118
Color Therapy, 56
Concentration, 31, 85
Confidence, 33, 55
Conjuration, 32, 47
Conjuring, 39, 45
Conscious Mind, 31
Conscious Will, 23
Consciousness, 18
Consecrate, 98
Consecrated, 94, 101
Consecration, 95, 112
Contemplation of God, 60
Controlling Energy, 49
Copper, 59
Correpondence, 95
Correpondences, 90, 95, 101 - 102,
118

Memory Retention, 127
Mental Magic, 67 - 68, 79
Mercury, 59
Merlin, 29
Metaphysical, 38, 49
Metaphysics, 7
Metronome, 129
Michael, 56, 59, 83
Microcosm, 37, 38 - 39, 45, 47
Mind, 27, 52, 85
Mindset, 25, 40
Mini Ceremony, 67, 68, 69
Miracle, 39
Miracles, 14, 38
Modern Physics, 37
Money, 60, 87, 91, 112 - 113
Money Spells, 87
Money Talisman, 101
Moon, 58, 93, 96, 98
Musk, 61
Myrrh, 60
Myth, metaphysical, 45

N

Name(s) of God, 58, 61, 81, 83 - 84
Needy People, 66
Negative Influences, 77, 81, 100
Negative Programming, 12
Negativity, 75, 77
Netzach, 56, 59, 89, 94
New Age Music, 99

O

Olibanum, 59
Operation(s), Magical, 27, 29 - 30
Opposite Sex, 135

P

Pain, 133 - 134
Pearl, 60
Pentagram, 80 - 84, 119

Personal Demon, 119
Personality, 47, 53, 110
Personality Trait, 47
Personality, the magician's, 45
Planet, 60
Playing Cards, 71, 107
Poltergeist, 114
Polyester (and Magic), 31
Positive Energy, 51
Possessed, 116
Power, 30, 47, 93 - 95, 98, 109
Power of the Mind, 67
Powers, Magic, 23
Premonition, 71
Principles (of Magic), 35
Programming, 11, 15
Promotion, 38
Pronounciation, 62
Protection, 91, 135
Psyche, 116
Psychiatrist, 116 - 117
Psychic Energy, 52
Psychic World, 58
Psychologist, 117
"Psychotronics" Tapes, 129 - 130
Psychosomatic Illness, 40

Q

Quabala, *see Kabbalah*

R

Rafael, 56, 82
Raphael, 59
Ratziel, 61
Real Life, 24, 27
Real Magician, 29
Reality, 24, 27, 38, 47
Reason, 19
Regions, the four, 55
Relaxation, 69
Releasing Energy, 111
Religion, 18

Rider-Waite Deck (Tarot), 107
Ritual, 84 - 85, 87, 97 - 98,
118 - 120
Rituals, 75
Robe, 29 - 31, 60, 85
Rose, 59, 78
Ruby, 60

S

Salvation Army, 66
Sapphire, 60
Science, 37 - 38, 56, 59
Secrecy, 30
Secret Language, 18
Secret Sign, 94
Security, 55
Self-Hypnosis, 68 - 69, 80
Seraphim, 60
Severity of God, 60
Sha-dai El-Chai, 58
Shy, being, 45, 47
Shyness, 117, 120
Sixth Sense, 71
Slow Breathing, 133
Spell, 24, 56, 62
Spell Book, 45
Spells, 32, 46 - 47, 90
Spirit, 47, 57, 80 - 81
Spirit World, 43, 118
Spirits, 7, 32, 43, 45, 53, 58, 65,
75, 99
Splendour, 59
Split Personality, 45
Star of Solomon, 18
Star Ruby, 61
Strength, 46, 60
Stress, 33, 68, 126 - 127, 134
Strorax, 59
Subconscious, 11, 13, 15, 17, 19,
20, 29, 35, 38, 46, 47, 62, 84, 89,
94, 101, 105 - 106, 124
Subliminal, 11, 13, 15

Subliminal Message, 95
Subliminal Programming, 12
Subliminal Tapes, 11
Success, 21, 31, 55, 123
Success, financial, 60
Successful, 9, 12
Sun, 59
Sundown, 96
Sunrise, 96 - 97
Sunset, 97
Super Brain, 20, 23 - 24, 31
Supernatural, 7
Symbol, 19 - 20
Symbolic Messages, 35
Symbolism, 15, 17, 29, 46, 57,
61 - 62, 67, 81, 109 - 110
Symbols, 17 - 18, 29, 33, 47, 53,
57, 62, 72, 89, 107

T

Talisman, 23, 46 - 47, 89, 91,
93 - 95, 97 - 101, 110 - 112, 121
Talismans, 62, 73
Tarot Cards, 71, 103, 105, 107
Technique(s), 63, 65, 69
Technology, modern   126, 128
Temple, 31 - 32, 58, 78
The Magus, 95
"Theta" State, 130
Thoth Deck (Tarot), 107
Tin, 60
Tipharet, 56, 59
Tithing, 65
Tobacco, 60
True Magic, 25, 39
True Magician, 24
Turquoise, 61
TV Preachers, 65, 66
Tzadkiel, 60
Tzaphkiel, 60